Priesthood Renewed

THE PERSONAL JOURNEY OF A MARRIED PRIEST,
ARCHBISHOP EMMANUEL MILINGO

BY ARCHBISHOP EMMANUEL MILINGO

Copyright © 2006 Archbishop Emmanuel Milingo

Bible versies in this book are taken from the New American Bible and the Jerusalem Bible

ISBN 10: 1-931166-27-7
ISBN 13: 978-1-931166-27-0

Printed in the United States of America

10 9 8 7 6 5 4 3 2

CONTENTS

PREFACE

I AM DELIGHTED TO offer a few words as a brief intro-
duction to this book of writings by Archbishop Emmanuel
Milingo which pertain to the *Married Priests Now!* Prelature.
It gives me great pleasure and honor to do so because Archbishop Milingo is an outstanding, prominent churchman
and pastor. He is widely known for his courageous defense
of African culture and tradition. And he is known for his
pastoral work as a preacher who does healings and exorcisms. His writings on the spiritual concerns of his African
people have brought them comfort and healing.

Last week, I attended the Erasmus Lecture in New
York City and the speaker was Dr. Philip Jenkins, a noted
professor of history and religion at Pennsylvania State
University. Professor Jenkins has written two books about
the Christianity of the Global South (Africa and South
America). He spoke about the impact of Holy Scripture on
the African Christian. In the question and answer session, he
was asked about Archbishop Milingo and his response was
very informative and very positive. He said that Archbishop
Milingo's message of healing and exorcism was exactly what
the Africans needed then and now because of their belief
in hereditary evil and sin. Archbishop Milingo's healing

ministry of exorcisms was the correct and best spiritual medicine the Africans could have received. He said that Archbishop Milingo's books and writings are immensely important to African Christians and will be for many, many years to come. When I spoke to Dr. Jenkins privately after the lecture, he opined that marriage would become a normal part of the ministry in the Global South because it is an important part of the expectations of the people.

When I think of the *Married Priests Now!* movement, it reminds me of the Solidarity Movement in Poland, when Lech Walesa united the working people into a movement that changed history and won freedom.

Married Priests Now! is such a movement. It is going to change church history and win freedom from obligatory celibacy. First, *Married Priests Now!* will unite the married priests and their organizations, and then it will gain the full acceptance of the people and the church. The other married priest organizations such as CORPUS, the Federation of Christian Ministries, CITI and others have been very cooperative and supportive, and we appreciate their help and advice. We honor their years of dedication to married priests.

St. Francis also changed the church when he founded a mendicant order of preachers which was far from the mainstream of the then opulent church. When Francis wrote the rule of the order, he wasn't concerned if it would gain the pope's approval. He knew that his movement was happening with or without papal approval.

And so it is with *Married Priests Now!* The married priests' movement is happening before our eyes because the people are reaching out and accepting the ministry of thousands of married priests in the United States and around the world *right now*. Thousands of married priests are being asked to perform weddings, conduct funerals and baptize babies on a regular and continuing basis. The people are not waiting for Vatican approval and are not concerned about it. This is the right time and the movement is happening and it cannot be stopped.

This year alone several new books are dedicated to the topic of married priests, namely, *Married Catholic Priests*, by Anthony P. Kowalski, which gives a history of the married priesthood, their journeys and their reflections; and *Freeing Celibacy*, by Donald Cozzens, which clearly shows that obligatory celibacy hinders the ministry of the church today. Periodicals like *CORPUS Reports* and *Diaspora* continue to edify and inspire married priests and their wives and families. Peter Manseau's book, *Vows*, and Simone and Corita Grudzen's not yet released film, *Immaculate Confessions*, also contribute to the collection of married priests' life stories.

In these pages, Archbishop Milingo offers his voice for the cause. Much more needs to be said and much more will be said on this vital topic. The forced obligation of celibacy as a requirement for the priesthood is unjust and inhuman and needs to be discussed by the laity and by the professional theologians – and by the hierarchy.

Archbishop Milingo is dedicated to the cause of a married priesthood and to the re-integration of married priests to full sacramental ministry in the church. His writings in this book show his own deep spirituality and his true concern about sacramental theology. He knows that a priest is a priest forever and that church-imposed restrictions cannot dismiss the priesthood. We have in Archbishop Milingo a Good Shepherd, a Good Samaritan, ready to take on the institutional Roman Catholic Church which has thrown away its priests without pensions or health care and without any concern as to what happens to them. He is not afraid of excommunications, penalties, punishments or threats. He knows that nothing can separate him from the Church or from his ministry to preach Jesus and Jesus alone. He remains a Roman Catholic Archbishop and will work to restore health and wholeness to the priesthood and to the church.

I admire what Archbishop Milingo is doing to renew the priesthood and to restore the priesthood to its scriptural authenticity. I thank him for his courage and selflessness in this new ministry, which may be his most important. May his words here encourage, heal and comfort the married priests and their wives and families because the families have also endured the sufferings caused by the Church's attitude towards marriage and the priesthood.

Peter Paul Brennan
Roman Catholic Archbishop
Married Priests Now! Prelature
DDamdg@aol.com
October 22, 2006
West Hempstead, NY
Married Priests Now!
web site: http://www.orgsites.com/ny/married-priests-now/
E-Group: http://groups.yahoo.com/group/MarriedPriestsNow/

INTRODUCTION

PRIESTHOOD STANDS ON ITS own, without celibacy as reinforcement. In the old priesthood of the High Priest Aaron, of the family of Levi, even the nature of this priesthood demanded a superior way of living. The perfection of priesthood is in its own nature. It is written that the priests of the Levitical order were the Lord's special company. They were not to own any part in Israel, except for the cities that were given to them by the different tribes to dwell in. The Lord was to be their entire inheritance. (Deut. 10:8-9; 18:1-8; 21:5. Joshua 13:14)

Gwen R. Shaw, on the matter of the Levitical priesthood, says:

> They were chosen to set a perfect example before all of Israel by keeping His Word and His Covenant, to offer the sacrifices and to teach the judgment and the law. They had to put incense before the Lord and offer

whole sacrifices on the altar, withholding nothing for themselves. They were never given an inheritance. God said: "I will be the inheritance of Levi."

The detachment from property, which relates to the "inheritance" in the Levitical priesthood, was the pouring together of the fruits of the work of the first Christian community. We read as follows: "The whole group of believers was united, heart and soul; no one claimed for his own use anything that he had, as everything they owned was held in common." (Acts 4:12)

Gwen R. Shaw describes the daily occupation of a Levitical priest as follows:

> He is called to be a mediator between God and man. He not only offers up the sacrifices to God, he is called to be a sacrifice himself. He has a lifetime of service before him. (*The Tribes of Israel*)

Marriage must never be an impediment to living according to what God wants of us. It had been believed that marriage would reduce a priest to a carnal level of concupiscence, and he would be numbed by carnal pleasures. What wicked thoughts!

The ministerial priesthood into which we are calling the married priests to reinvest themselves takes its integrity and wholeness from the One who made it so, God the Father who planned it. As you can see, there is no mention of celibacy.

However, in between the Levitical priesthood and the priesthood of Jesus, there is the Melchizedek priesthood. How strange that the Melchizedek priesthood is far higher than the Levitical priesthood! The humility that Abraham, in whose loins was Aaron, the future high priest, displayed to Melchizedek by giving him a tithe of one tenth of each of his possessions indicates that Melchizedek was superior to Abraham. Moreover, Melchizedek was a mysterious figure. It is said that he had no father and no mother, and nobody knew where he came from.

Why then was Jesus compared to Melchizedek? Because Jesus too is a mysterious figure, God-man. But He is higher than Melchizedek, because it is God Himself who ratifies His priesthood by an oath. He ratifies the eternity of His priesthood.

The superiority of the priesthood of Jesus has two important constituent elements. One is that it is God the Father who swore that Jesus was consecrated and appointed priest by God Himself. The second element is that He was priest forever, that is, in eternity. And this is the priesthood we enjoy. King David expresses it in Psalm 110:4: "Yahweh has sworn an oath which He never will retract, 'you are a priest of the order of Melchizedek, and for ever.'"

Our priesthood is tied with that of Christ and Melchizedek:

> The figure of Melchizedek serves as means of reflecting on the meaning of Christ: Priest and King, who, bringing forth bread and wine, blessed Abraham. We are called to share in the priestly reality of Christ, partaking of the bread and wine which form the ongoing celebration of our Covenant with God Most High, who loves us and draws us to himself, through

the priestly mediation of Jesus Christ. (Michael G. Witczak, S. J.: *Dictionary of Biblical Theology*)

The late Holy Father, His Holiness John Paul II, says:

For this reason, on Holy Thursday we, the "ministers of the New Covenant," gather together with bishops in the Cathedrals of our local churches; we gather together before Christ – the One and Eternal source of our priesthood.

The family as a domestic church together constitutes a community of priests. Hence we read in Isaiah, God foresees that Israel, when well settled, will give glory and praise to God. They will offer not only sacrifices but their whole life; as a community they will raise their voices to God, glorifying Him as their Father and Creator. By so doing, as a nation, they will act as one single priest does on behalf of the community. Hence Isaiah says: "The people I have formed for myself will sing my praises." (Isaiah 43:21)

St. Peter in his first letter calls us Christians to be aware of the shared priesthood from Jesus. This is what the Vatican Council II divided into two: the ministerial priesthood, that is, the ordained minister, and that of the Christian community. Hence St. Peter says in his letter: "Like living stones, let yourselves be built into a spiritual house to be a holy priesthood to offer spiritual sacrifices acceptable to God through Jesus Christ." (1 Peter 2:5)

The married priest's family becomes "a living stone," which upholds the members as priests from whom sacrifices are continuously being offered for the expiation of their own sins and for those of the community. There is in this family both ministerial priesthood and the royal priesthood as a chosen family to serve God and the community in a special way. The married priest's family should be conscious of this fact, much more than the other members of the Christian community. They share in the priesthood of the head of the family, the husband, while combining with their own "royal priesthood" received from Christ, the head of the family of Christians.

Let us work hard to bring back the true face of a Christian family, the Holy Family. They were all holy. The married priest's family has all the elements necessary to live more closely the true life of the Holy Family of Nazareth. It is beyond doubt that Mary, the Mother of Jesus, and St. Joseph her husband, truly shared in the priesthood of Jesus. So would the whole family of the married priest.

Archbishop E. Milingo

Press Conference at the National Press Club, Washington, D.C.

PART I
Press Statements

Married Priests Now!
Statement

JULY 1, 2006

MARRIED PRIESTS ARE LONGING
TO SERVE THROUGH THE CHURCH

IT IS VERY CLEAR that the Roman Catholic Church has a great need of priests. The bishops worldwide have brought their concern repeatedly to the Vatican. In addition, priests are needed to bring the Eucharist to those Catholic people who do not have a resident priest. The Eucharist is the essence of Catholicism.

Currently on the sideline, there are approximately 150,000 validly ordained priests. But these priests are married. The majority of these priests are ready and willing to return to the sacred ministry of the altar.

It is our mission to find a way to reconcile these married priests with the Church and to reinstate them in the public sacred ministry, working in every way possible with the Church.

It is evident that the "care of souls" demands a new pastoral provision to make this vision a reality.

No lesser apostle than St. Paul himself demonstrated his theology of the priesthood and the episcopacy when he wrote to Timothy:

> A Bishop must be irreproachable, married only once, temperate, self controlled, decent, hospitable, able to teach, not a drunkard, not aggressive, but gentle, not contentious, not a lover of money. (1 Timothy 3:2-3)

Married priests are longing to serve God and the people in the Christian community through the Church. The new association of married priests called "Married Priests Now!" is calling for those priests who are currently married, along with national and international married priest organizations, to unite in an open call to the Roman Catholic Church to reconcile married priests to active service. Archbishop Milingo feels that he is an apostle called to bring married priests back to full service in the Church due to the current priest shortage and the need to bring the Eucharist to every Catholic.

Archbishop Milingo wants to see a priest in every parish. He feels it is the Will of God to bring priests back as full, vibrant and active ministers of the word and Eucharist.

Married Priests Now! wants to value the ministry of married priests and reconcile them to public sacred ministry. It is not only a benefit to the Church but to all of humanity. The role of the married priests in the family is essential. The family is the nucleus of the Church and of society. The priest's ministry to his family gives him the experience and relationship to see the gospel differently and practically.

The charisma of married priests is needed now. St. Peter was a married priest, and so were the other apostles. It is the right of every human person to freely be accepted and given in marriage. This right must be returned to priests in the Latin Roman Communion. It is not only a matter of justice to the priesthood but also a matter of the survival of the Church in the future.

For further information about Married Priests Now! please call 202-577-3544.

Statement by His Grace Archbishop Emmanuel Milingo

NATIONAL PRESS CLUB, WASHINGTON, D.C.

JULY 12, 2006

THE END OF MANDATORY CELIBACY!

Ladies and Gentlemen,

WE ARE DEALING WITH a very serious matter that has affected the Catholic Church for many years. In the last 35 years since the International Catholic Synod of Bishops in 1971, the struggles surrounding celibacy have worsened. If in 1971 the Church had listened to the appeals of the bishops to offer celibacy as an option to those who would bind themselves to it for their entire lives, but let those called to be ordained priests, yet married, fulfill their calling, then today we would not be harvesting straw instead of divine graces.

The seriousness of the matter was emphasized once again when the U.S. bishops raised the issue as we entered this third millennium. Once more, the authorities in the Vatican waved it off, to the detriment of the Church in the USA and around the world.

Married priesthood has existed as early as the time of Moses, for we read in Leviticus that all the family of the High Priest Aaron were married. Some argue that what was demanded in that priesthood was merely a legal purity. But when God demanded sanctity as a sign of being intimate with Him, this injunction of sanctity was still more applicable to priests: "Be holy, because I, your Lord, am holy." Sanctity or holiness is the first requirement of any priesthood, married or celibate.

The apostles ordained priests and bishops, regardless of their marital status. St. Paul ordained Timothy and consecrated him to bishopric. He ordained the first bishop of the Island of Malta, who was a married man. As St. Paul said to Timothy, the one condition he imposed upon a bishop was to marry only once.

A Bishop must be irreproachable, married only once, temperate, self controlled, decent, hospitable, able to teach, not a drunkard, not aggressive, but gentle, not contentious, not a lover of money. (1 Timothy 3:2-3)

Some people will be surprised to hear what became of Zaccheus, the short man whom Jesus called down from a sycamore tree and then visited in his house. He truly was converted with his whole family, and ended up being consecrated bishop of Caesarea Philippi. (Venturi: *History of the Church*)

JESUS AND HIS APOSTLES

Jesus shared fully with all His apostles, both married and non-married, all that was required to be an apostle. He did not show favoritism to any of them. Even as He gave them responsibilities, He looked to each one's capacity and relied on each of them. The question of celibacy was not His preoccupation. I think that the demands presented by St. Paul to a candidate to bishopric are more than sufficient for the life of a bishop. Looking back to priesthood, from which rank a bishop comes, the same demands are applied to the priesthood.

AN OPEN CALL

We hereby appeal to those bishops who have been sent to the monasteries, condemned forever, never to be a pastor or appear any more to their faithful. Let them come out of their Catholic prisons and be reinstated, taking once more their pastoral responsibility among the married priests. Please let us know where you are; be in contact with us.

To those priests who may feel that by marrying they have stepped down or fallen short: unleash your burden of humiliation, isolation and shame. Come among your fellow "sinners," so considered, who were to be branded, and to be forgotten forever as weaklings. Come in, but never come with lamentations. Your burden has been taken away; you come light, released from any weight of sinfulness. Become a Magdalene, a Paul, a Peter or Augustine, or one of the many others who never looked back to their struggling past.

They all became outstanding saints, in spite of their former weaknesses.

To our beloved "Mother Church," we beseech you to open your arms to these prodigal children who have longed to return home and have so much to offer. There is no more important healing than the reconciliation of 150,000 married priests with the Mother Church, and the healing of a Church in crisis through the renewing of marriage and family. The Church has nothing to lose by allowing priests the option to marry. Historically, out of holy marriages have come priests, popes, saints and loving servants of God and the Church.

It is out of our love for our faith and deep concern for its future that we proclaim this day, the end of mandatory celibacy, and the option for priests to sanctify the family as it was intended in the Garden of Eden, even as they fulfill their calling and ordination.

May the abundant blessings of God be upon you all.

Part II

Milingo and Married Priesthood

Letter to Married Priests Now!

Emmanuel Milingo

Washington, D.C., United States of America

July 16, 2006

My Dear Brothers, Married Priests Now!

PEACE OF CHRIST, AND greetings from Washington, D.C. Our meeting is over. I am certain that you have heard through TV, radio or newspaper all that we have discussed together. Our document, the conclusion of the meeting, from to July 12-14, 2006, has been diffused in 165 English newspapers and 110 Italian papers. We know that publishers of papers in many other languages have given our statement ample space in their papers. We owe them all a big thank you.

A few have taken it upon themselves to threaten us with excommunication or laicization. These are words that became obsolete after Vatican II. Nor can they be used for our case, because we are not quarrelling with anyone. We are stating facts, which are pungent in the lives of married priests. Excommunication and laicization are unnecessary threats, which we consider, as the Lord says, to be "using old bottles for new wine." Only a stingy person will do so. But he will lose clients later on when they realize that he uses old bottles for new wine.

The married priests are always priests. They have an indelible priestly character, "according to the order of Melchizedek, the eternal priest." This indelible character cannot be "excommunicated or laicized." So is Jesus the Eternal Priest, He too according to the order of Melchizedek. "No one takes this honor upon himself but only when called by God, just as Aaron was. In the same way it was not Christ who glorified Himself in becoming High Priest, but rather the one who said to Him: 'You are my son; this day I have begotten you,' just as He says in another place: 'You are a priest forever according to the order of Melchizedek.'" (Hebrews 5:4-6) This truth of the indelible character of priesthood is as well repeated to us every Holy Thursday.

Our examination of a priest must not stop with how he looks as we see him as a human being. He is a valuable person before God and before the holy people of God. St. Ambrose puts it well when he says:

You saw the Levite there, you saw the priest, you saw the High Priest. Do not consider their outward appearance, but the grace of their ministries. It was in the presence of Angels that you spoke, as it is written: "the lips of a priest guard knowledge and men seek instruction from his mouth, for he is the angel of the Lord of Hosts." (*Roman Breviary*: St. Ambrose on Mysteries)

My dear brothers, married priests, it is true that through a long period of dispassion, despair and many other aspects of your suffering you have been inclined to assume that you became unwanted by the Church. But now once more through this circular you have been evaluated from the nature of your priesthood. Those of you who are able to gather together into threes or fives, please pray together as priests' families or celebrate Mass together. Bring back Jesus in your midst and in your community. Be available if a local diocese asks for your priestly services.

God bless you and be with you.

Yours sincerely,

Archbishop Emmanuel Milingo

Circular II

My Lord-Bishops and Married Priests,

DO NOT THINK THAT you will get a circular every week. This second circular has soon followed the first because of its urgency and the development of our association, "Married Priests Now!" After we received many positive responses, the advisers to the association met on August 10, 2006, and they unanimously agreed that this second meeting of married priests was appropriate and had to take place soon.

We hereby announce to you the good news that we expect 130 priests in Washington, D.C., at the Sheraton Hotel, arriving on Sunday evening for those who are from countries like USA and Canada. Others may arrive on Saturday depending on your airlines. We will have supper together on Sunday. After supper, there will be a social gathering. The meeting is scheduled for Monday and Tuesday, while Wednesday is the departure day.

Please, send us your passport identification details; we shall issue your tickets, which will be consonant with your passport information. Please, do not delay getting your visa for the United States. If you send us your identification details, we shall send a personal letter of invitation from our association.

Very important announcement! Please, bring with you an alb and a stole for the celebration of Mass. For those who will arrive Saturday, we shall celebrate Mass together on Sunday morning at the hotel. Cleanse your souls from all grudges created by the circumstances that led you to your actual state that have caused you a lot of pain. You are no more a wounded soldier in the army of Christ. Like Saint Ignatius of Loyola, wake up and go to the Holy Land to follow the footsteps of the wounded Jesus, the triumphant and the risen One. We are going to share the gifts of our resurrection with the whole Church. We are married priests with a difference; Jesus has told us to "wake up now and watch with me. Let us go to meet the enemy." Ours will be holiness acquired from the purification of our souls as we underwent the agonies, which took different forms. The Blessed Virgin Mary is in the forefront leading us back to Jesus, the High Priest. Together with Her we rejoice for our double parenthood, human and spiritual, the new symbols of victory of the Roman Catholic married priesthood.

Very important note: Please tell us how many married priests will come from your area or nation. Remember that we will have a limited number for this second meeting. We can accommodate 130 (one hundred and thirty) married priests.

Looking forward to meeting you.

Yours respectfully,

Archbishop Emmanuel Milingo

Circular III

My Dear Married Bishops and Priests,

IT WAS NOT MY intention to send you a third circular so soon. However, due to the impression I had when I read the directory of the Corpus Association of married priests, I once more pushed up my sleeves in order to work harder for "Married Priests Now!" You, as priests, have received in life more than ten talents. But remember that the ten talents had to be doubled. When I saw your academic qualifications, your availability in the service of humanity cannot just be watered down because you have opted to marry. I congratulate you for the many initiatives you have undertaken in order to help one another. I therefore invite you to resume the services in the Church from your cherished vocation, and once more be the priest that God intended you to be.

We are now going to hold our second meeting September 17-19. Here is the good news. I was first invited to have a dialogue in Lugano, Switzerland, on a neutral ground, so he said. The invitation came from a prelate with a high post in the Vatican. But I did not accept the invitation because I did not feel that going back to Europe was safe for me.

Today, September 7, I had an official visit by the Auxiliary Bishop of Washington Diocese. Together with Archbishop Stallings, we presented to him the aim of our organization. The Auxiliary Bishop told us that he was only a representative of the Archbishop of Washington and that the archbishop himself wants to meet us for a dialogue on the matter. We have asked him to meet us before September 17, and we proposed to him that the Archdiocese of Washington, where we reside, send a delegate or an observer to our meeting.

This is a step further in our movement. We are glad that the initiative comes from the Church. We shall hold our dialogue before September 17, 2006. Please, pray for a good outcome and mutual understanding. That is why we feel that the September 17-19 meeting should accommodate 120 married priests. We all have but one desire and aspiration:

"To remain married priests and serve the Church as Catholic married priests."

It may seem from the outset that the suffering and humiliations endured by our married priests have been unbearable, but not to all. One priest did not want to say the word "Catholic," but after our first meeting, he understood that there might have been other priests who have suffered more than he did. He has changed since then and has addressed married priests in four cities in Italy, where he was so courageous as to tell them about our organization. We look forward to his sharing with us his new experience. He has as well appreciated our circulars and other documents from our office, which deal with married priests. In the forthcoming meeting, we shall speak together with one voice to reclaim our priestly ministry. We have to, because the Catholic Church cannot afford such a loss of so valuable personnel to her subsistence.

Let the words of St. Peter Damian and the prayer of the Church on his feast be my own for you:

> My dear friend, you begged me to write you a letter to comfort you and by kindly encouragement to sweeten the bitterness of your soul in the many trials that you are enduring.

From the many e-mails we have received, what St. Peter Damian is writing to his friend is the experience of the majority of the married priests, if not all. However, I would like to invite the married priests to pray with the Church on the feast of St. Peter Damian as follows:

> Almighty God, teach us by the example and doctrine of St. Peter Damian to prefer nothing whatsoever to Christ, and to make the service of your Church our chief concern, and so come to the joy of your eternal Kingdom. We make our prayer through our Lord Jesus Christ. Amen. (*Roman Breviary*)

I would like to conclude on a note that may sound sentimental. I have been curious why the Blessed Virgin Mary calls priests "My Priests." The story begins from far away, from the birth of Jesus Christ. It is strange that the Fathers of the Church compare the transubstantiation of the bread into the body of Christ and the wine into the blood of Christ as the work of the Holy Spirit, which it is, and they relate it to the overshadowing of the Holy Spirit on the Blessed Virgin Mary for the conception of Jesus.

It is true that in both cases it is the Holy Spirit at work. Thus we can conclude that a priest, as he celebrates Mass, repeats the action of the Motherhood of Mary. Truly, Mary presented her Son Jesus to the Magi, who were pagans, and to the shepherds, who represented the poor and the many who were waiting for the Messiah. So also the priest, as he raises the consecrated Host and the transformed wine into blood in the chalice, is introducing Jesus once more to the whole of humanity. This continuous repetition of presenting Jesus to the world makes the Church remain a sacrament of salvation to the whole world. A sacrament is always a sign of God's mystical presence among the people. The Word of God, the Holy Scripture is, according to the Fathers of the Church, the first sacrament, as Jesus Himself says: "My words are spirit and life." The Fathers of the Church put the Eucharist as the second sacrament, as a sign of salvation.

Let me take a direct quotation from St. John Damascene:

> Should anyone ask, "How is the bread changed into the body of Christ?" I answer: The Holy Ghost over-shadows the priest and operates through him that which He operated in the sacred womb of Mary. (Lib. 2, C. 14)

The Greek Fathers agree with St. Augustine in this teaching. But in many points they don't accept his views. I personally see a lot in his statement with regard to the

32

dignity of a priest, and he too points out a similarity with the Blessed Virgin Mary. He says:

> O venerable and sacred dignity of priests, in whose hands as in the womb of the Virgin, the Son of God is incarnate every day, O stupendous mystery which God the Father and the Son and the Holy Ghost perform through the priest in so wonderful a manner. (*De dignitate Sacerdotum*)

St. John Chrysostom touches the sense of the eternal priesthood of Jesus. He sees the altar on which a priest celebrates Mass being present in heaven. A priest is *"alter Christus,"* and as he celebrates, the Heavens participate. Thus he says:

> Heaven has nothing, absolutely nothing more than earth; earth has become a new Heaven. Go up to the gates of Heaven, or rather go up to the Highest Heaven; look attentively, and I will afterward show you an altar that which struck you more than anything else in Paradise.

There is another reason why the Blessed Virgin Mary calls priests "My Priests." Jesus Himself recommended John the apostle as the son of Mary: "This is your Mother," then to Mary: "This is your son." John was both an apostle and a priest. Thus rightly so does the Blessed Virgin Mary call priests "My Priests." They are a continuation, not only of the mission of Christ, but also spiritually related as Mother and Son in the work of salvation.

Look at the 150,000 married priests put on the shelf. Look at the possible achievements they would have attained. That is why we have to renew the priesthood and give it what is due to it. Let us work at it.

God bless.

Yours sincerely,

Archbishop E. Milingo

Archbishop Emmanuel Milingo and his wife at their Marriage Blessing in Washington D.C., 2001.

September 17-19 Married Priests Now! Convocation, NJ.
Archbishop Emmanuel Milingo giving the welcoming speech.

Concelebration of Mass during the Married Priests Now! Convocation.

Circular IV

My Dear Married Priests,

WELCOME BACK TO YOUR homes after our second meeting in New Jersey September 17-19. I am addressing even those married priests who sent e-mails when they heard of our meeting in New Jersey. Though you did not come, we thank you for accompanying us with your prayers. We hope you will do all you can to not miss the next meeting, which we shall soon announce.

I would like to share with you the result of our meeting. By the act of coming together, each one of us loaded with a curse of condemnation, through communality and communion, the heavy burden was removed. As we prayed together and celebrated together, our human dignity returned to ourselves. Through the free sharing with everyone around us, what was condemnation became a reason for fraternal unity.

More than once voices were raised though even here, having brought our wives with us, the voice of a woman was lacking. Not many of the women raised their voices. Certainly, they were happy to speak through their husbands. We ended up at the concluding lunch by announcing that a special convocation, entitled "A Convocation of Women Married to Priests," will be our next meeting. But the theme will be studied by them, and presented by them. We look forward to the convocation. It will be time that the men will learn to listen to the wisdom of women.

Though taken up by the freedom and ease and the welcoming attitude of everyone towards everyone, both men and women lamented the lack of personal prayer. On the other hand, the majority did not know that there was the Eucharist in the opposite room. There was no written sign announcing the presence of Jesus in the Eucharist. However others also felt that the celebration of Mass filled in many of those personal devotions, such as the rosary, the forgotten breviary, "since I was reduced to a lay state."

We thank our master of ceremonies, Father Joseph. The details of community prayer will be included in our next program: a recitation of one or two Psalms as a morning prayer before Mass. Our prayer life ought to come back into our daily activities. We belong to God and to the community.

We are the past, belonging to the true Church of Jesus Christ, with full apostolic foundations. More than one remarked, "But why did these priests not say Mass?" The Mass as it was said was not changed, not in the least. It was celebrated as designed and renewed by the Vatican Council II. Of course, we are Catholics in all aspects, except that we are Catholic married priests.

Where Do We Go from Here?

The most important aspect of our convocation as married priests is the meeting. It is here where we confess to one another what hurt us in life, without omitting confessing as well how we offended or scandalized our neighbors. By being faithful to come to the meetings, we are acquiring knowledge to update ourselves and to learn to share our experiences. So never miss our meetings. That is how we have kept the past, the Church tradition.

The present is the convocation itself, which puts us in contact with "birds of the same colors"; we share common burdens. We also come to learn that our burden was exaggerated as we lived alone, hardly sharing it with anyone; we are glad to hear consoling words of encouragement. We learn to admire the virtuous life of our brothers and sisters.

Our future is in our hands. Here we are. We are shaping it, a community of married priests now. Each one of us is a full member. This is your community, and my community. In our conversation with friends, be it at work or in our social gathering, let us have courage to say, "I am a Catholic married priest." This was the normal Church pattern from the beginning of the Church. The other was an exception, and only a few are meant to take it as their way of life. We are living this life, and we are saying it. It is our belief. If the Church will say it tomorrow, let it be. But we are saying it now, and we are convinced it is so.

The Family Mass

The Mass in its nature is a family gathering and celebration — the agape, a moment of sharing brotherhood and sisterhood. Our new community of Married Priests Now! should keep the celebration of the Mass alive. Our family celebration takes twenty-five or thirty minutes. This can be done once or twice a week, if possible, till the Mass comes back in our midst. As I proposed in the first circular, if I remember well, I also mentioned a possible celebration together with families who live nearby each other. Our members, having endured all the consequences of alienation of their priesthood, as they become members of our association, "Married Priests Now!" are hereby released from all entanglements to their priesthood and can therefore practice their pastoral work. Some have shown that they have not been affected by the condemnation by the fact that they have found ways and means to carry on their pastoral work.

My brothers and sisters, you are released from all bondages which condemned you without a tribunal. May God put to your merit your sufferings, and reward you with forgiveness. Raise up your head, praising the Lord for His mercy.

Archbishop E. Milingo

Circular V

Let Us Talk Together in Honesty

WE HAVE NO REASON up until now, my dear married bishops and priests, for regretting having washed our dirty linen in public. In all our documents, we have shown respect and reverence for the Church. Due to the name of our Catholic Church, upheld so high in the eyes of the world, if we, the married priests, have been the cause of the slow motion within the Church, which has led to the loss of her reputation, by our action to reinstate the married priests we have taken one of the greatest steps to restoring the good name to the Church.

You are surprised that I do not bring you to a Church tribunal for having married while you were in your pastoral field. What you did was an offense, which was attached to your change of mind through your impulse and discovery of who you were. You longed to be with someone outside, a partner in a true human union through marriage. That law was only a precept attached to your priestly vocation. You opted to lead a natural life in matrimony. Some of you, considered by your superiors as angels, could not easily be allowed to put away your vow of celibacy. All the same you gave it up, and with it your pastoral priestly ministry was taken away.

We understand that this precept does not deserve to be called law. Human nature itself has expressed itself in these days, and human experience has rejected it. From the overwhelming number of e-mails from all over the world, we have come to understand that celibacy is no longer a necessary attachment to priesthood. Debates are still going on in the whole world. We have only been an opportunity through which finally the world has voiced its hidden opinion on the matter. It means that the precept was implicitly imposed on the candidates to priesthood, without offering them an option. As they presented themselves as candidates to priesthood, they were made to believe that it was a requirement to embrace priesthood. As a matter of fact it was not so. Priesthood stands on its own, without celibacy as reinforcement.

The New Priesthood

In the old priesthood of the High Priest Aaron, of the family of Levi, even the nature of this priesthood demanded a superior way of living. We must admit that human nature, however, has always diminished the luster of God's calling in nearly every human vocation. Starting with the Christian family, it is said that sixty percent of the Christian families in the world are standing either on one leg or completely paralyzed, that is, living in misunderstanding and unforgivingness, or divorce. What a pity! This is the case of the actual priesthood. To delay in calling the priests to the original standard of priesthood, be it the Levitical priesthood or that of Melchizedek, is to participate in wearing away out the true meaning of priesthood.

The perfection of priesthood is in its own nature. It is written that the priests of the Levitical order were the Lord's special company. They were not to own any part in Israel, except for the cities that were given to them by the different tribes to dwell in. The Lord was to be their entire inheritance. (Deut. 10:8-9; 18:1-8; 21:5. Joshua 13:14)

Gwen R. Shaw, herself a Jewess, helps us to put clearly the demand of priesthood as God put it to the chosen family of Levi. We are tracing the roots of our priesthood. Marriage must never be an impediment to living according to what God wants of us. It is useless to come back to our prior celibate priesthood, lost externally through our marriage, by refusal to go by the law, a law which did not give us an option. As we embrace once more our ministerial priesthood, let us show love for our vocation and uphold the high standard to which we were originally called. It had been believed that marriage would reduce a priest to a carnal level of concupiscence, and he would be numbed by carnal pleasures. What wicked thoughts!

Going back to Gwen R. Shaw on the matter of the Levitical priesthood, she says:

They were chosen to set a perfect example before all of Israel by keeping His Word and His Covenant, to offer the sacrifices and to teach the judgment and the law. They had to put incense before the Lord and offer whole sacrifices on the altar, withholding nothing for themselves. They were never given an inheritance. God said: "I will be the inheritance of Levi."

A Spanish journalist asked me: "How will you support your many married priests? They have to maintain their families. That is why the Church preferred celibate priests, who, when they die, none of their relatives can claim anything." If this be the case, we have the more reason to take away mandatory celibacy. The Church should not sacrifice the lives of the priests for a little money, which a priest will have in his bank account when he dies. Then celibacy has been bought at too much of a price that has cost the lives of many priests.

The second reason for not approving the illogical sacrifice of priestly celibacy because of a material reason is the fact that the Church did not preserve the way of life proposed by the first Christian community. The detachment from property, which relates to the "inheritance" in the Levitical priesthood, was the pouring together of the fruits of the work of the first Christian community. We read as follows: "The whole group of believers was united, heart and soul; no one claimed for his own use anything that he had, as everything they owned was held in common." (Acts 4:12) Hence, says Gwen R. Shaw, "They were never given an inheritance, God said, 'I will be the inheritance of Levi.'"

We are not going to be impeded from realizing the designs of God, which have been announced to us through the Blessed Virgin Mary. I am certain that the Association, Married Priests Now!, will overcome this material difficulty.

We just need to use some of our own priests to study seriously how to adhere to what the Lord says in Leviticus of His own people, the priests, whose full-time devotion is well set forth. The Lord will Himself care for those who will be working full time for the whole community of Married Priests Now! Gwen R. Shaw describes the daily occupation of a Levitical priest as follows:

> He is called to be a mediator between God and man. He not only offers up the sacrifices to God, he is called to be a sacrifice himself. He has a lifetime of service before him. (*The Tribes of Israel*)

The ministerial priesthood into which we are calling the married priests to reinvest themselves takes its integrity and wholeness from the One who made it so, God the Father who planned it. As you can see, there is no mention of celibacy. God did not demand a so-called first-class sacrifice of "celibacy," as it has been believed up till now. "The Levites are a people with the high calling of God upon their lives."

We, who have suffered for the second choice of our lives, married life, should no more lower again in any way the white linen of priesthood.

Let us see why our actual priesthood has jumped from the Levitical family to the family of Judah. The Judah blood lineage does not have such good origins attached to it. But here for the sake of Jesus, who purified the blood lineage of Judah, we are settled in peace and enjoy the same nobility as Jesus.

However, in between the Levitical priesthood and the priesthood of Jesus, there is the Melchizedek priesthood. How strange that the Melchizedek priesthood is far higher than the Levitical priesthood! The humility that Abraham, in whose loins was Aaron, the future high priest, displayed to Melchizedek by giving him a tithe of one tenth of each of his possessions indicates that Melchizedek was superior to Abraham. Moreover, Melchizedek was a mysterious figure. It is said that he had no father and no mother, and nobody knew where he came from.

Why then was Jesus compared to Melchizedek? Because Jesus too, is a mysterious figure, God-man. But He is higher than Melchizedek, because it is God Himself who ratifies His priesthood by an oath. He ratifies the eternity of His priesthood. As to the unclear origins of Melchizedek, Jesus enjoys the same. "Who are you?" The question came from the crowd. "Why do you hide yourself?" they asked Him. "You do not know where I come from," He replied. Thus he was an unknown figure, hard to understand.

The superiority of the priesthood of Jesus has two important constituent elements. One is that it is God the Father who swore that Jesus was consecrated and appointed Priest by God Himself. The second element, not less important, but equally important, is that He was priest forever, that is, in eternity. And this is the priesthood we enjoy. King David expresses it in Psalm 110:4: "Yahweh has sworn an oath which He never will retract, 'you are a priest of the order of Melchizedek, and for ever.'"

The Dictionary of Biblical Theology's discussion on Christ's priesthood, which is ours, ties our priesthood with that of Christ and Melchizedek in a nice and smooth way, as follows:

> The figure of Melchizedek serves as means of reflecting on the meaning of Christ: Priest and King, who, bringing forth bread and wine, blessed Abraham. We are called to share in the priestly reality of Christ, partaking of the bread and wine which form the ongoing celebration of our Covenant with God Most High, who loves us and draws us to himself, through the priestly mediation of Jesus Christ. (Michael G. Witczak, S. J.: *Dictionary of Biblical Theology*)

The late Holy Father, His Holiness John Paul II, said:

> For this reason, on Holy Thursday, we, the "ministers of the New Covenant," gather together with bishops in the Cathedrals of our local churches; we gather together before Christ – the One and Eternal source of our priesthood.

Married Priesthood: The Totality of Priesthood

The family as a domestic church together constitutes a community of priests. Hence, we read in Isaiah, God foresees that Israel, when well settled, will give glory and praise to God. They will offer not only sacrifices but also their whole life; as a community, they will raise their voices to God, glorifying Him as their Father and Creator. By so doing, as a nation, they will act as one single priest does on behalf of the community. Hence, Isaiah says: "The people I have formed for myself will sing my praises." (Isaiah 43:21)

St. Peter in his first letter calls us Christians to be aware of the shared priesthood from Jesus. This is what the Vatican Council II divided into two: the ministerial priesthood, that is, the ordained minister, and that of the Christian community. Hence St. Peter says in his letter: "Like living stones, let yourselves be built into a spiritual house to be a holy priesthood to offer spiritual sacrifices acceptable to God through Jesus Christ." (1 Peter 2:5)

The married priest's family becomes "a living stone," which upholds the members as priests from whom sacrifices are continuously being offered for the expiation of their own sins and for those of the community. There is then in this family both ministerial priesthood and the royal priesthood as a chosen family to serve God and the community in a special way. To make it clear, let us refer to what Elaine M. Wainwright writes in her article in *Colleville Pastoral Theology*. She writes as follows:

> The totality of the lives of the members of these communities then become like "sacrifices" within the temple of God's presence in the world (Romans 12:7). In the words of St. Paul, Romans 12, we read the following: "Think of God's mercy, my brothers, and worship him, I beg you, in a way that is worthy of thinking beings, by offering your living bodies as a holy sacrifice, truly pleasing to God." (Romans 12:1-3)

The married priest's family should be conscious of this fact, much more than the other members of the Christian community. They share in the priesthood of the head of the family, the husband, while combining with their own "royal priesthood" received from Christ, the head of the family of Christians.

Let us work hard to bring back the true face of a Christian family, the Holy Family. They were all holy. The married priest's family has all the elements necessary to live more closely the true life of the Holy Family of Nazareth. It is beyond doubt that Mary, the Mother of Jesus and St. Joseph her husband, truly shared in the priesthood of Jesus. So is the whole family of the married priest.

Archbishop E. Milingo

Archbishop Emmanuel Milingo and his wife at the American Clergy Leadership Seminar Dinner, NJ, September, 2006.

Circular VI

Married Priests Now!

My Dear Married Priests,
Peace of Christ.

I WOULD LIKE YOU to remember that in your lifetime someone like Father Damian, the leper priest of Molokai, who dedicated his life to the lepers till he too became a leper, so should you consider me as one of you, marrying and dedicating my life to you married priests. The Church is unable to conceive the change of my life, and still more to accept my new state of life as "a married priest."

Let me make it very clear to you. I cannot put together my belief in the duty of loving all and saving all (Acts 28:28; John 17:26) while closing my eyes to the mental tortures and moral degradation of a rejected priest who has fallen in love with a woman. For the sake of the good name of the Church, his crime is punished, not by a punishment equal to the crime committed, but by a lifetime of humiliation to the priest. For the rest of his life he leads a life of a fish out of water. That is leading a life of which he had never dreamt. As a matter of fact, a Catholic priest who breaks the vow of celibacy is considered a shame to the Church. In the whole Church, he is considered a sexual weakling and a shame in the Catholic Christian community. His children are categorized as illegitimate and have a special appellation such as "the son or daughter of a priest," which means the fruit of a priestly adultery. I have e-mails on the matter which would fill more than 150,000 books, more than the recorded number of married priests themselves.

What I don't understand is the attitude of the Catholic Church towards such an issue, which is consuming the life-stem of the Church itself. Is it true that celibacy is more valuable than the life of the priests themselves, who are supposed to embrace it willingly? In the course of a thousand years, there have been all sorts of tentative ways to cover up the sins of priests. But now, in my observation and opinion, the Catholic Church prefers to go on covering up the priestly sins against celibacy with their consequences, because the good appearance of the Church must be maintained. But this is at the cost of the loss of many souls, who find themselves victims of scandals, which they cannot accept from a Church so noble and respected as the Catholic Church.

The good name of the Catholic Church comes from the good name of the founder, Jesus Christ. And the priestly vocation is built on holiness. The change of mind of a priest, who marries after years of celibate life, should be treated not as a failure in life but rather as another God-given status in life. They should thank him for what he did for many years and send him back into the world as a married priest. He deserves a send-off with a blessing and best wishes for his new state of life.

Priestly Sins Prolonged by Maintaining Celibacy

Celibacy has become an ideal in the Catholic Church. It is a sign of superiority over all the Christian churches. It is believed that pure saints come from celibacy. The celibate saints will be far above the married people, who are qualified as mere laity by following the celibate priests from afar. I believe that their pride in this concept has prolonged the existence of crimes of priestly celibacy in the Catholic Church. The luster and the poetic beauty of the so-called Angelic Virtue, alias celibacy, are maintained as a trophy of the morally strong in the Catholic Church, while the real fighters for high morality are the married priests, who have to maintain their own individual moral integrity and the communal family duties with their different character and personalities. To be a saint in a family environment requires a lot more fighting against personal ego and faithfulness and perseverance to carry on one's family duties. A married man has to carry the daily cross from within his own family as well as his inter-relationships with the world outside.

How is it that we are not discussing the issue of celibacy? The fight against me to return to my status as a celibate priest blinds those who love me and keeps them from looking closely at the issue we are dealing with. We are saying that celibacy should be optional. It has already surpassed the limits of the benefits it was supposed to bring to the Catholic community. It has consumed its own fruits, which have become briars and sour grapes.

If we take into consideration the different forms of crimes committed during the struggle to maintain celibacy, the number of saints who emerged out of celibacy is by far smaller than the number of fallen priests. The side products from within the walls include homosexuality and pedophilia. There are many others, which are scandalous and horrible, not worth mentioning in a public and open conference such as this one of ours. What I said earlier, that celibacy has consumed its merits, I would like to make clear by an example.

> The bees in the cold season cannot go out to collect pollen from flowers. They are locked in by the cold. Hence, they begin to eat their own honey, without leaving anything for the future.

What I mean is that throughout the thousand years of celibacy, sexual sins committed by celibate priests slowly crept in. Now it is clear that the harm this causes is taking the form of a shortage of priests. Thus, celibacy has eaten up its babies, just as some animals do as soon as they give birth. In such a case, the owners have to remove the little ones from the mother for a certain period. But celibacy has continued eating priests for over one thousand years, and now we are running short of priestly vocations.

The matter at hand has been called a useless clamor based on the impression made by those who claim that it is devastating to the Church, which is a fact. It is not good to look at the poor personality of those who are presenting the matter. God has often used those who are fools in the eyes of the world to increase the confusion of the wise, stirring them to believe. To begin to condemn us and analyze our personalities is to lose sight of the contents of the matter at hand, optional celibacy.

Yours, loving as ever can love,

Archbishop E. Milingo

Circular VII

October 20, 2006

Bowing to the Shouts of the Crowd

ONE CANNOT UNDERSTAND AT all what the shouting crowd wants until the voices slowly fade away and silence is achieved. At such a moment there is a need to set up means of control and bring about order by allowing single voices to be raised. A journalist once wrote that Milingo raised so much dust and now all is passing away; people are taking what he says "*cum grano salis,*" with precautions, not swallowing all that he says.

As a matter of fact, not all of those who usually shout in the crowd are courageous enough to raise their voice when only their voice may be heard; it takes courage to keep shouting even if in the end there is only one voice. When all is quiet, then one feels, "they will listen only to my voice." To be certain of what one wants to say, regardless of the possible adverse consequences, takes courage and conviction.

The story of celibacy, which occupies such a noble place in the Roman Catholic Church, should be looked at with courage and objective analysis. Celibacy has led the Church into a spiritual deficit; something is lacking. I am not talking of money. Truly the Roman Catholic Church should put on mourning clothes to weep both over the priests who are lost or fallen, and over the incredible number of victims who had to suffer in order to preserve the external coating of celibacy. The tide of sex scandals has risen so high that it is "drowning" the Roman Catholic Church into a dungeon of shame.

They call me proud and sexually infatuated. When it comes to the change of mind that is needed on the matter of celibacy, the Roman Catholic Church is the "PROUD ONE." I categorize the pride of the Catholic Church like that of Pilate. I look at two moments in Jesus' life when all was in Pilate's hands. The wife of Pilate had warned him not to do anything with "the life of this innocent man, Jesus." He seemed to have accepted his wife's dream and so washed his hands. But when Jesus gave a true statement of who He was, Pilate did not accept the truth from Jesus' mouth. He asked, "What is the truth?" But before Jesus answered, Pilate stood up and went away.

They say I am proud. If they say that, it should be based on what I have written regarding celibacy. However, they take into consideration only their own belief that I am out of my wits, that I am no more myself. I understand that they love me, but in order to understand the change that I have undergone it is important to understand my new language and my new role in the life of the Catholic Church. What is the issue? Is mandatory celibacy not a problem in the Catholic Church today? They do not even read with care what I have written about celibacy.

The second aspect of Pilate's pride shared by the Roman Catholic Church is Pilate's lack of firmness when he had an opportunity to treat Jesus justly. If Jesus had had the opportunity to speak at length with him, Pilate would have understood Him and possibly defended Him, following the word his wife had sent him. However, by standing up and going away without waiting for the definition of the truth, he failed.

Now let us see his firmness at the death of Jesus. He wrote on the cross, "Jesus of Nazareth, King of the Jews." The Jews protested. They did not accept Jesus as their king even after His death. But now Pilate showed his authority and firmness by declaring to them: "What I have written, I have written." Jesus needed Pilate's firmness and courage while He was struggling for His life. It was up to Pilate to defend and save His life.

Today the Catholic Church is saying the same thing regarding the mandatory celibacy imposed on future priests at the Council of Trent (1545–1563): "What they wrote, they wrote."

Celibacy was proposed in the Council of Elvira (305–306) but was not easily accepted. Bishops brought cases of failures of celibacy to Pope Gregory VII, and in 1073 he firmly imposed mandatory celibacy. Then at the Council of Trent it was officially ratified as a distinctive mark of the Roman Catholic priesthood.

Are we not playing with the precious lives of priests when we put them in situations that history has proven to be old wine bottles? What does this firmness profit the Roman Catholic Church? Today, we her children are ashamed. We no longer hold our heads high as celibate priests, because people know that we are not what we say we are. Whom are we pleasing by saying that we are celibate when as a matter of fact we are not? The Roman Catholic Church receives the honor but pays the cost in loss of membership. We don't want to mention those who lose even their faith in God due to the sex scandals which are going on in the Roman Catholic Church.

LEAVING THE 99 AND GOING FOR THE ONE THAT IS LOST

This is a very well-known parable where Jesus gives value to an individual person. Leaving the ninety-nine and going to look for the one solitary lost sheep has a lot of significance. This one sheep that got lost blocks the round number 100 from achieving "fullness." Here "fullness" means completion; but it cannot be achieved, because "one less will always leave emptiness in a whole." In His mission to save, Jesus will not rest till everyone is saved. This is what the second Vatican Council says: "The Word of God, through whom all things were made, was Himself made flesh, so that as a perfect Man He could save all men and sum up all things in Himself." (Vatican II: The Church in the Modern World: N. 40, 45)

Looking at the Church in the United States of America, it is no longer a secret that the greatest problem they are facing is the problem of sex scandals. The Vatican, the headquarters of the Catholic Church, received a warning as early as 1961 when Cardinal Spellman presented the problem to His Holiness Pope John XXIII. Nothing was done. Then in 1971, the synod of Bishops presented the matter to the Holy See, but again it was considered one of those problems that had to be put on the shelf, and so it was.

What I don't understand is what I have quoted earlier from the Vatican II statement on the importance of salvation for everyone. The married priests are the objects of salvation. They cannot go on leading a life that does not guarantee their salvation. On the other hand, the Church has the mission of Christ who goes out to look for the one individual who is lost, leaving the ninety-nine at home. Is the Catholic Church satisfied with the ninety-nine celibate priests and chases away the one who has lost the way to celibacy? Is he to live as such till the end of his life, without the Church going out to look for him?

Let me go back to the Vatican II, the Church in the Modern World. Herein again universal salvation is clearly emphasized. And of course we all know that charity begins at home. The Catholic Church needs to look into its family before it extends a helping hand to the rest of the world. Vatican II: "While helping the world and receiving many benefits from it, the Church has a single intention: that God's Kingdom may come and that the salvation of the whole of humankind maybe achieved." (*Op. cit.*)

LAICIZATION

This is a false doctrine and a lie to the ignorant public. We are made to believe that a priest can be reduced to laicization, or to a lay state. The nature of priesthood is such that through consecration a human being is lifted up into another state of responsibility of his life, so that what he has become touches his being. For instance, it is said that if by misfortune a Christian who is validly baptized, anointed and consecrated to God goes to hell, the devils torture him the more because of the sign of baptismal consecration by which he renounced Satan, his works and his pomps. A Christian cannot in any way become a pagan. So also an ordained priest is a priest throughout his life. He will be so even in the other life.

When a priest has been reduced to a lay state, he is the first one not to believe it, especially when the reason is because he has chosen marriage. He feels that he has made a choice that is natural to him. But on the other hand, he does not understand why he cannot continue to be a priest. Many so-called laicized priests have died feeling unfulfilled in life because of the fact that they had been deprived of the exercise of their priestly ministry.

The Light, the Yeast and the Salt of the Earth

I would like to turn to the married priests and humbly ask them to forgive all those who have been involved in their actual suffering condition. The words St. Polycarp used to teach the clergy of his time are still valid and applicable to us. He said: "If we pray to the Lord to forgive us, we ourselves must be forgiving; we are under the eyes of our Lord and God, and everyone of us must stand before the judgment seat of Christ, where each will have to give account of himself."

In calling married priests back to active ministry, we want them to be once more "the new salt, yeast and light." Thus we must believe that a new opportunity is being given to us to resume the activities of our priestly life. We leave behind the old man and put on the new one, Jesus Christ, the priest, the Eternal priest. There is no doubt at all that those who ceased to work as priests ten years ago, for instance, will feel the change of atmosphere in the environment in which they were working. Changes have taken place. This is in many ways what causes misunderstandings in the Church itself. The problems which a priest of today comes across cannot be solved by the theological theories of yesterday. The priest of today ought to be sufficiently informed of the actualities of the problems and do all he can through inspiration and human experience to arrive at the required answer. "As for the clergy," says St. Polycarp, "they should be men of generous sympathies, with a wide compassion for humanity. It is their business to reclaim wanderers, keep an eye on all who are infirm, and never neglect the widows, the orphans, or the needy." It is in these situations that a priest learns the human situations today.

A life of prayer will help a married priest to offer daily to the Lord the needs of his people and never feel like a man out of place. By living with people and listening to them, he will get sufficient up-to-date information to satisfy his audience. He will solve many of their problems. They will then call him their priest.

Archbishop E. Milingo

Part III

Bishops: Consecration and Call to Action

Apostolic Succession and Married Priests Now! Prelature

APOSTOLIC SUCCESSION IS A key element in the role of the bishop and the church because it shows a clear and vibrant link to the early Church and to the Apostles. My apostolic succession flows from His Holiness, Pope Paul VI, who consecrated me. By the consecration of four bishops who like the apostles were married, I have now passed on that apostolic succession to the Married Priests Now! Prelature.

Apostolic Succession is the belief of the Roman Catholic Church that Jesus commissioned the apostles to establish a church. He sent the Holy Spirit upon them at Pentecost and said that He would be with them until the end of time through the work and action of the Holy Spirit in the Church. The apostles called others to ministry by laying hands on them and invoking the Holy Spirit in prayer to consecrate them for ministry in the church. By this action the apostolic succession of the apostles through the Holy Spirit was transferred to or passed down to the new bishops. And this is what I did when in full mental and physical capacity, I ordained four bishops for our Prelature.

Some want to say that I have been brainwashed or that I was under the influence of medicine or drugs when I consecrated these bishops so that they can call it a defective consecration. This is far from the truth. I personally planned the consecrations, conducted the practice beforehand, and celebrated the ordination ceremony itself with great care, dignity and accuracy according to the Roman Pontifical. The consecrations were videotaped and shown all over the world via Italian television transmission. I gave a lucid, clear and enthusiastic interview on American television immediately following the ordinations. I have been brainwashed but **only** by the Gospel of Jesus Christ and by the faith and tradition of the Holy Roman Catholic Church which I love and profess daily. I am a Roman Catholic Archbishop and I will be so all the days of my life. I was at the moment of the consecration in full mental and physical vigor and capacity, and I continue to be so today. I acted in complete personal freedom and was not in any way constricted or compelled by any outside agent, person or organization. I acted with the same freedom and integrity as the Holy Father does when he consecrates bishops. The married men I consecrated are validly consecrated bishops, and are Roman Catholic Archbishops in good standing with the Married Priests Now! Prelature. Our Prelature is and remains part of the One, Holy, Catholic and Apostolic Church.

Holy Orders in the Church and in our Prelature has three levels: deacon, priest and bishop. Apostolic Succession in holy orders applies to all three levels of priesthood but usually only a bishop traces his lineage or line of succession. It is generally said that all bishops can trace their lineages back to the apostles. If a bishop can trace his succession in orders to a pope or well-known patriarch, cardinal or metropolitan archbishop, that is usually sufficient to show that he has apostolic succession. In theory, apostolic succession can be traced back to the apostles, but in practice because of non-existent records, it is difficult to go beyond the Middle Ages for most successions.

In the third century, Tertullian wrote: "Have you an Apostolic Succession? Unfold the line of your Bishops." Thomas C. O'Reilly, writing in the *Catholic Encyclopedia,* makes the following comments on Apostolic Succession:

> Apostolicity is the mark by which the Church of today is recognized as identical with the Church founded by Jesus Christ upon the Apostles. It is of great impor-tance because it is the surest indication of the true Church of Christ, it is most easily examined, and it virtually contains the other three marks, namely, Unity, Sanctity, and Catholicity. Either the word "Christian" or "Apostolic," might be used to express the iden-tity between the Church of today and the primitive Church. The term "Apostolic" is preferred because it indicates a correlation between Christ and the Apostles, showing the relation of the Church both to Christ, the founder, and to the Apostles, upon whom He founded it. "Apostle" is one sent, sent by authority of Jesus Christ to continue His Mission upon earth, especially a member of the original band of teachers known as the Twelve Apostles. Therefore the Church is called Apostolic, because it was founded by Jesus

Christ upon the Apostles. Apostolicity of doctrine and mission is necessary. Apostolicity of doctrine requires that the deposit of faith committed to the Apostles shall remain unchanged. Since the Church is infallible in its teaching, it follows that if the Church of Christ still exists it must be teaching His doctrine. Hence Apostolicity of mission is a guarantee of Apostolicity of doctrine. St. Irenaeus (Adv. Haeres, IV, xxvi, n. 2) says: "Wherefore we must obey the priests of the Church who have succession from the Apostles, as we have shown, who, together with succession in the episcopate, have received the certain mark of truth according to the will of the Father; all others, however, are to be suspected, who separated themselves from the principal succession," etc. In explaining the concept of Apostolicity, then, special attention must be given to Apostolicity of mission, or Apostolic succession. Apostolicity of mission means that the Church is one moral body, possessing the mission entrusted by Jesus Christ to the Apostles, and transmitted through them and their lawful successors in an unbroken chain to the present representatives of Christ upon earth. This authoritative transmission of power in the Church constitutes Apostolic succession.

Holy Scripture speaks of the role of a bishop in 1 Timothy 3:1-7:

This saying is trustworthy: whoever aspires to the office of bishop desires a noble task. Therefore, a bishop must be irreproachable, married only once, temperate, self-controlled, decent, hospitable, able to teach, not a drunkard, not aggressive, but gentle, not contentious, not a lover of money. He must manage his own household well, keeping his children under control with perfect dignity; for if a man does not know how to manage his own household, how can he take care of the church of God? He should not be a recent convert, so that he may not become conceited and thus incur the devil's punishment. He must also have a good reputation among outsiders, so that he may not fall into disgrace, the devil's trap. (*New American Bible*)

The following chart of my apostolic succession is adapted from the listing of my consecration as a Roman Catholic Bishop which appears on this website: http://www.catholic-hierarchy.org/bishop/bmilingo.html

EMMANUEL MILINGO, Metropolitan Archbishop of Lusaka in Zambia. Consecrated 1 August 1969, Kololo Terrace, Kampala, Uganda, by Pope Paul VI, Giovanni Battista Montini, assisted by Sergio Pignedoli, Titular Archbishop of Iconium and Secretary of the Evangelization of Peoples, Roman Curia, later Cardinal-Deacon of S. Georgio in Velabro, and by Emmanuel Kiwanuka Nsubuga, Metropolitan Archbishop of Kampala, Uganda and later Cardinal-Priest of S. Maria Nuova.

This succession includes Popes Paul VI, Pius XII, Benedict XV, St. Pius X, Clement XIII, Benedict XIV, Benedict XIII, and through Archbishop Milingo's co-consecrators Pius IX, Pius VIII and Cardinal Merry del Val.

Archbishop Emmanuel Milingo (1969)

Pope Giovanni Battista Enrico Antonio Maria Montini † (1954)

Eugène-Gabriel-Gervais-Laurent Cardinal Tisserant † (1937)

Pope Eugenio Maria Giuseppe Giovanni Pacelli † (1917)

Pope Giacomo della Chiesa † (1907)

Pope St. Giuseppe Melchiorre Sarto † (1884)

Lucido Maria Cardinal Parocchi † (1871)

Costantino Cardinal Patrizi Naro † (1828)

Carlo Cardinal Odescalchi, S.J. † (1823)

Giulio Maria Cardinal della Somaglia † (1788)

Hyacinthe-Sigismond Cardinal Gerdil, B. † (1777)

Marcantonio Cardinal Colonna † (1762)

Pope Carlo della Torre Rezzonico † (1743)

Pope Prospero Lorenzo Lambertini † (1724)

Pope Pietro Francesco (Vincenzo) Orsini de Gravina, O.P. † (1675)

Paluzzo Cardinal Paluzzi Altieri Degli Albertoni † (1666)

Ulderico Cardinal Carpegna † (1630)

Luigi Cardinal Caetani † (1622)

Ludovico Cardinal Ludovisi † (1621)

Archbishop Galeazzo Sanvitale † (1604)

Girolamo Cardinal Bernerio, O.P. † (1586)

Giulio Antonio Cardinal Santorio † (1566)

Scipione Cardinal Rebiba †

Archbishop Emmanuel Milingo at the Married Priests Now! Convocation.

Archbishop Emmanuel Milingo with Archbishop George Augustus Stallings

Episcopal Consecration Mandatum

THIS IS TO CERTIFY that I, Archbishop Emmanuel Milingo, was ordained priest by Bishop Firmin Courtemanche of the Missionaries of Africa, popularly known as White Fathers of Africa, on August 31, 1958, at St. Mary's Mission, Diocese of Chipata, Zambia.

Eleven years after my priestly ordination I was unanimously elected by the Zambia Episcopal Conference to become Archbishop of Lusaka. During the Papal tour of Africa in 1969 to the Shrine of the Martyrs of Uganda, together with eleven other bishops-elect, I was consecrated Archbishop of Lusaka by His Holiness Pope Paul VI, assisted by Sergio Cardinal Pignedoli and Emmanuel Kiwanuka Cardinal Nsubuga.

Having been equipped by this apostolic character from the consecration I received from His Holiness Pope Paul VI, I now invoke this same apostolic power and authority to consecrate my beloved brother bishops,

Peter Paul Brennan
Joseph Gouthro
Patrick Ernesto Trujillo
George Augustus Stallings

as bishops of the Holy Roman Catholic and Apostolic Church in the Married Priests Now! Personal Prelature.

Given on Capitol Hill in Washington, District of Columbia, on this 24th day of September, the year of our Lord 2006.

+ Archbishop Emmanuel Milingo,
Metropolitan Archbishop Emeritus of Lusaka

Consecration of the Bishops.

October 1, 2006

Most Reverend Archbishops and Bishops of Married Priests Now!

PEACE OF CHRIST. I am hereby congratulating you on the day of the Octave of your consecration. Ours is a new office given to us by Our Lord Jesus Christ, sanctioned as well by His Mother, the Blessed Virgin Mary. This night, October 1, 2006, the Lord Jesus Christ showed me the great crowd of people who will adhere to our mission. I do not know as to whether we are the suitable people to carry out His plans. However, ours is to dedicate ourselves to the task given.

These are some of the demands from the Married Priests Now! Association, by which you ought to abide. I know that each one of you came to be where you are by your own initiative. Thus it is clear and well understood that you are attached to your own spiritual baby. Without intending to arouse scruples in your consciences, I want only to know how you feel, up to what extent you can dedicate your time and yourself to the cause of Married Priests Now! Please, let each one of you tell me his limits or extent to which he will share his life with our infant organization.

We are failing already, in spite of you all being Americans. You, as the citizens of America, can you not find a way to register this Association? The more we delay, the more people will change their minds and believe that by presumption we embarked on a task to which we were not equal. We have been pulling the legs of the people. We can begin in a small way by renting a small office, to which each one of us will subscribe for its maintenance. It is good to start with difficulties in a humble way. Then God, seeing us failing to raise even a penny for the rent of our office, will act.

His Eminence a German Cardinal of an inter-religious church in Germany, having heard that I was excommunicated, invited me to join them. He did not know that I am at a crucial moment, where I must prove my determination to support and defend the married priests. I thanked him for the invitation, and as soon as possible, I shall certainly visit him and his community.

We have to come together soon and discuss the expansion of our association as well as to look deeply into what we mean by "a personal prelature." Will this answer the question of incardination? What is involved in setting up "a prelature"?

We have in the pipeline two big families of Old Catholics. One is in the Philippines, with bishop-elect candidates, expecting to be consecrated by us. This has to take place as early as the beginning of the year 2007. Then by the end of this year, 2006, we ought to consecrate five or seven bishops of the Old Catholic Rites of Portugal, Angola and Czechoslovakia. This needs a lot of Roman Catholic understanding of the history of the Old Catholic Rite.

We must state publicly that as they are consecrated by us, anything they acquired as black sheep from the Catholic Church falls away. Why does the Catholic Church claim to reinstate Episcopal Consecration and bring them truly back to the Mother Church? Ours is a need for a deep study of both theology and history. Those of tomorrow will not be able to defend themselves without looking deeply into what we are doing. We are setting up a great task for them.

God bless.

Yours most respectfully,

Archbishop E. Milingo

October 3, 2006

My Dear Bishops and Archbishops,

I WOULD LIKE TO share with you some of my impressions and even shock caused by these e-mails. After your consecration, the Lord opened the world to us, the "Married Priests Now!" The majority of the e-mails we have received completely overlooked the so-called "excommunication." Only a few people who are certainly not versed in Church affairs have sent negative responses and reactions to the work carried out by poor me on you on September 24, 2006.

I therefore urge you to act quickly, as they say, "Strike while the iron is hot," in such a way that we may not regret later on that we did not know the time when the Lord was passing by. I see our role as a continuation of the work of the late Holy Father John Paul II. That is, he asked pardon to the whole world on behalf of the Catholic Church for the crimes committed against humanity and against the churches. We felt at home with every religious denomination, as he paved the way to brotherly love and unity.

The reactions from our separated Brethren to the consecration of the four of you are beyond our expectation.

I personally see it as the fruit of the strenuous efforts of reconciliation into which His Holiness Pope John Paul II invested all his heart. Just to take one example, let us look back to what he did as he united the youth of the whole world. They felt he belonged to them. As he died, the youth came to pay homage to him, and they wept as they would weep for their own blood fathers.

It is impossible to believe that our separated Brethren, without God's touch and motion, could invite us to consecrate their bishops-elect. They do not believe in the excommunication, the language of the Roman Catholic Church. They only see God's finger in what we have carried out on September 24, 2006. Those waiting for Episcopal Consecration are four groups:

1. Portugal and Angola
2. England, Wales and Ireland
3. Philippines: Group A
4. Philippines: Group B

What has affected me most is what our correspondent in England said: "Come to help us, as scattered as we are in small religious denominations. Bring us to unity. Just as well to expel the hesitations and doubts of the faithful on the validity of the sacraments we give them." What a task we have!

What is it that the late Holy Father John Paul II left undone? This is what our separated Brothers are demanding from us. It was to uproot the cause of conflict between other religious denominations, which made them break from us. We should put it this way: "He left them still under the yoke of condemnation." Today they are telling us that whatever caused friction, and consequently separation, should be taken away now through our consecration of their shepherds. So by consecrating them, we are completing the work of His Holiness Pope John Paul II.

Thus, in accordance with the Gospel of John, Chapter 10, we read: "And other sheep I have, which are not of this fold: them also I must bring, and they shall hear my voice; and there shall be one fold, and one shepherd." (John 10:16)

I propose to have a separate meeting of bishop-leaders of those who are inviting us to consecrate their candidates. We would like to share with them in depth our concerns and our willingness to respond positively to the invitation. At this meeting, we shall look deeply into our mutual understanding, and establish new bonds for everlasting unity in love.

God bless.

Your most respectfully,

Archbishop E. Milingo

October 6, 2006

My Dear Bishops,

PEACE OF CHRIST. YOU might have an impression that I live only on writing. To your surprise I say this: I prefer to live in the presence of God and enjoy my life in God, just as the life of a fish finds its fulfillment in water. In order to understand what I write, I must read and re-read till I, like yourselves, slowly make sense out of what I have written. Most of what I write sounds to me like dictation.

I give you an example. Circular V, dated October 7, 2006, was rather smooth writing. After eight pages in my own handwriting, I felt from within me that something was not accepted by the Lord, Jesus Christ. I stopped and read the circular. Regarding Jesus as King and High Priest, with His priesthood not from the Levitical lineage but from Judah, I found out that the Lord Jesus did not want this point to be developed. He did not want us to look down upon a blood lineage that had had so many flaws in life. Hence I did not develop that part of His priestly lineage. Thus, I mentioned the mysterious origin of Melchizedek, who had no father and no mother, and asked where he received his priesthood.

The letter to the Hebrews insists on the superiority of his priesthood to that of the Levitical priesthood. His priesthood, therefore, was not consecrated by any blood lineage.

Hence, Psalm 110 of David gives Jesus both titles of priesthood. Jesus is a priest with the same mysterious nature of priesthood like that of Melchizedek; His is just as eternal as that of Melchizedek. The New Testament priesthood is, therefore, of a mysterious origin, and it is eternal.

Consecration of the Four Is Valid

Please follow my reasoning. You must be the first ones to believe that what I did was valid. The validity on my part has been proved by the fact that if what I did was sinful, the Lord Jesus Christ would have been the first to blame me, just as He did not want me to go deep into the priestly blood lineage of Jesus, if examined through the line of Judah and, of course, of David, His Ancestor. If what I did to consecrate you would have led me to madness, because it was to be a grave and serious sin, who would forgive me under the sun?

Melchizedek, without father or mother, exemplified the future figure of Jesus, having a mother, yes, but not through a human seed but instead through the intervention of God Himself, the Holy Spirit. Then comes the *materia prima* of the new priesthood, "bread and wine." Has God ceased to achieve His ends? Not at all!

The Matter Is Excommunication

Someone wrote me as follows on October 3, 2006. In what he is saying, he is touching the question of a mandate. I am just letting you see what other people led by God say on the matter:

> Our Lord Jesus Christ tells me to inform you that the law of excommunication is spurious and unreal as far as the supreme law of salvation (*suprema lex "salus animarun"*) is concerned. This is in Canon 1752. When one is excommunicated for cooperating with Jesus Christ of Nazareth in the saving of souls that excommunication does not hold at all: it is non-existent. It is null and void. Love covers many sins. Taking the risk to obey God and Jesus Christ His only begotten Son in one's life shows one's true love for God and Jesus Christ. One becomes a hero or a heroine for God and His affairs, and therefore a saint or martyr. (Matthew 10:34)

If ever there is in anyone of you some doubt of what I have done, rest assured that I, as your single consecrator, had a mandate from Jesus. It may be that one of you, or more than one, began to have some remorse. However, you should have a consultation with me. If it were a small matter, I would say, "*Ecclesia supplet*," not "*Papa supplet*."

Let me share with you just a little of who I am. "The spiritual implications in the holy name 'St. Mathias,' is that you Archbishop Emmanuel Milingo are going to be used by Jesus Christ Himself to save His Holy Church from bad apostles (e.g., bishops and priests) who use some issue in the Holy Church such as celibacy to cover themselves as they lead sinful lives, e.g., Masonry, sex and homosexuality or in general devil worship and Satanism in the Holy Church of Jesus Christ. Surely you are the Great Apostle Mathias, my Reverend Archbishop Emmanuel Milingo." But such messages are not to be shouted about on the rooftops. On my part what I did, I did it right. You should not have any doubts at all.

What We Are Aiming at with Married Priests Now!

I know that if the plans of God to work for Married Priests Now! are to be realized, you have somehow to lose some of your feathers. When the seer spoke of *"salus animarum"* at stake, it is truly business and God's business. Certainly when He calls someone to carry out His will, though He accompanies the one called with *"grazia status,"* He does not make it easy. He only supplies assurance of what one is called to do, and courage to fulfill His will. He does not work with a weakling who will crumble under the weight of the burden.

My stand is clearly in line with what the seer is saying, that is, "the salvation of souls is at stake." The married priests were the dry bones, left alone in the streets. For example, one priest who had been so shocked after being excommunicated by his bishop that he had abandoned even prayer or going to church, as soon as he came among us and celebrated Mass with us, he became alive. He shared his joy with us as he told us what had happened to him. You too certainly have other stories of married priests, which they shared with you during our two convocations. We are really engaged in the work of the salvation of souls.

Only the Pope Gives a Mandate

There are exceptions to some rules. The one I have quoted above, *"Ecclesia Supplet,"* is one. It does not say, *"Papa Supplet."* In the case of circumcision, Paul had to stand alone against all the apostles and the standing tradition of the Jews, the Law of Moses, as the sign of the covenant. In modern times, that would be "Baptism" as entrance into the family of the elect of God. So was circumcision. Paul and Barnabas won the battle and called the then Pope, St. Peter, to look into the problem.

They were Jews and had witnessed the wonders of what the grace of God does. With their conviction, they presented the matter of circumcision as not being necessary for the new converts, whose tradition it was not. Peter had to listen to them and later on accepted the proposed change. Someone must make the move. Today we have no circumcision as a requirement for salvation.

Is it easy to change tradition? I do not include celibacy in tradition when it has been inserted into the pipeline carrying with it the poison that has been slowly killing the life of the Church. We must feel the pain of Mother Church, who is giving birth to dead children, 150,000 and more married priests. It is to this vocation of salvation within the Church that we must dedicate our lives. If the overseers of the Church are unable to see it this way, we shall still go ahead until they see our work and finally approve it. God will continue to teach us how to go about it. We are at it; let us move.

Let me conclude with a consultation I gave to a seer, who answered by quoting a Bible verse: "On that day there shall be open to the house of David and to the inhabitants of Jerusalem, a fountain to purify from sin and uncleanness." I had asked about celibacy on September 19, 2005. The opening sentence of chapter 13 of Zachariah refers to: "The end of falsehood." It was already a problem for me. But I wanted to be sure that I do not act on my own personal conviction. Then on May 30, 2006, the Blessed Virgin Mary lamented the situation of her priests, which is us. So there was no more doubt that a way should be found to solve the problem. So we are at it now.

God bless.

Archbishop E. Milingo

October 11, 2006

My Dear Bishops,
Archbishop George Augustus Stallings
Archbishop Patrick Trujillo
Archbishop Peter Paul Brennan
Bishop Joseph Gouthro
My Dear Brothers,

I AM FORWARDING TO you a letter which I have received from Cardinal Giovanni Cheli from Rome. I want you to look at it immediately so that this evening, at the 8:30 conference call, we may share our thoughts and put together what we ought to answer. I am hereby translating the letter from Italian to English:

> My dear brother, in your letters I have read with profound pain and sorrow that you are preparing to ordain priests and bishops. I swear and appeal to you, please do not do it. You have always confirmed in words and writing that you will never do anything against the Church. But your actions contradict your words.

Remember that God has called you to be a shepherd in the Church and not a rapacious wolf, which kills and scatters the sheep.

My dear brother, I once more exhort you to think about death and the judgment before God as to what you are going to present to Him at that moment: if you think about the judgment before God, it is the only remedy to temptation of the flesh and of pride.

You do not want to serve the Church but to put yourself above the Church. You do not want to be guided by the Church but rather to impose on the Church your ideas and your will. Is this not diabolical pride? This is the last time I am writing you but I shall not stop even one moment from praying for you, together with the sisters and brothers whom you have founded and whom at this time you have seriously scandalized.

There are so many of us praying for you and supplicating the Lord so that He may open your eyes and that you may find the right way.

Your Brother in Christ.

Giovanni Cardinal Cheli

Married Priests Conference

September 17, 2006

My Dear Lord-Bishops and My Brother Priests,

IT IS NOT YET one month since we launched our association, Married Priests Now! We have so far received a lot more positive than negative reactions. One young priest from Hungary, a recently ordained priest still in his honeymoon of celibacy, sent in his high appreciation of celibacy and hence disdained our arguments for reinstating married priests in the Roman Catholic Church. We thanked his parents for not having chosen to be celibate; otherwise he would not have come into the light of the world. So many priests have come from holy families. It is the story of many saints.

On the other hand, we don't know who has put in the mind of many that we intend to abolish celibacy. With this understanding, they overlooked what we have said in our document, and so condemned us as rebels against the Catholic Church. Jesus Himself made it very clear, when the apostles heard Him say that marriage is indissoluble: "What God has joined together, let no one can put asunder."

The apostles, listening to Jesus defending marriage to such an extent that there was no possible way for divorce or separation, in this case preferred to remain single. Even here Jesus told them that it was only for those who were chosen to do so for the sake of the Kingdom. The disciples said to Him:

> "If that is how things are between husband and wife, it is not advisable to marry." But He replied: "It is not everyone who can accept what I have said, but only those to whom it is granted....There are eunuchs who have made themselves that way for the sake of the Kingdom of Heaven. Let every one accept this who can." (Matthew 19:10-12)

Marriage has its origin directly from God, while celibacy is an exception. Marriage by nature is divine, while celibacy is an option and for a few. It has become an imposition by the Catholic Church and has been inserted in priesthood as its essential constituent part, which it is not. In the whole Jewish traditional priesthood, there is no mention of conditioning priesthood with celibacy. The way Jesus defines marriage, even He as Son of God cannot divorce nor separate two people married before God. He says it in the following clear terms:

> He answered, "Have you not read that the Creator from the beginning made them male and female and that He said: This is why a man must leave father and mother, and cling to his wife, and the two become one body? They are no longer two, therefore, but one body.

So then, what God has united, man must not divide."
(Matthew 19:3-6)

Here is what St. Gregory Naziazeno says about marriage:

Il matrimonio e suggello di un affetto infrangibile, quelli che nella carne si uniscono fanno un anima sola e col loro mutuo amore insieme affilano la punta della fede, perché kil matrimonio non allontana da dio ma tanta più avvicina perché vi ci spinge Egli stesso. (Gregorio Naziazeno)

Paraphrased: "Marriage is a seal of an indestructible affection; those who are united in body form only one soul with their mutual love, and they arrive at such a point of faith, because marriage does not keep them away from God but rather God Himself brings them close together because He is the one who pushes them closer together." (Gregory Naziazeno)

Looking down on marriage must become the past history of the Church. The longed-for true renewal of the world should take its origin from marriage. As we have said earlier on, it is God who pushes the family into the forefront of humankind to take its proper position as the true bond of divine covenant. Here is what *Pastoral Dictionary of Biblical Theology* says:

There is a basic thrust throughout the Judeo-Christian tradition: "which says": people are not to live as isolated, individualistic entities, but as vibrant men and women, creatures of a loving God, relating to God, self, others and nature in ever-deepening bonds of justice and love.

Let me not dwell too long on marriage, since I am a neophyte in the camp. However, I have shared with you the little I know of the importance of marriage. You can rely on me on the matter of the value of marriage in human society. Maybe having come into the field so late, the spiritual value of marriage as seen from the divine viewpoint has more space in me than my other part that looks at sexuality through the one-sided upbringing of my scholastic days promoting the Angelic Virtue of celibacy.

Though I have passed over the other phase of vibrant sexuality, my whole self embraces the derivatives as fruit of the matrimonial union. I have come to understand literally: "It is not good for a man to be alone." If I had undertaken this task at the period of youthful sexuality, I believe that my reasoning powers through faith might have been diminished. The youthful sexual impulse could easily be considered to be the real motive for defending married priests. But now at my age, it is charity and love that push me to put all my efforts into defending the married priests, because I love them and their families, and wish them the best of life. I would like to be affirmed by our own Catholic teaching in the Catholic Catechism, which consoles me when I read the following:

The Genesis account of human origins, with much subsequent revelation, proclaims the divine origin and sacredness of human sexuality and its purposes, the divine institution of marriage, and the dignity and nobility of woman, who had been degraded in so many societies of fallen humankind. (*Catholic Catechism*, Man and Woman)

It is up to us as married priests to uphold marriage with all that it contains. Ours is an obligatory exposure of married life, as the ones who keep the traditional divine values of marriage. This is our newness as Catholic married priests to aim to the heights God has set to be attained, through the marriage bond of a man and a woman. We are going to show them that there was more hidden in marriage, which humanity has still to discover: that is, the completion of human nature. We are one soul and body, and we must believe it: we become one flesh through marital love.

THE GOOD SAMARITAN

Threats have not been lacking from those who wish us the worst that should befall us. As usual, they lack words, and the only word available is "excommunication." For two thousand years, those whom the Catholic Church truly excommunicated were those whom they put to death, and there are many on the list. Others became branches of Catholicism, not Roman Catholics. Today they too are churches to reckon with. The same Roman Catholic Church, during the Vatican Council II started calling them separated brethren, and their relationship with the Vatican is classified into what is known as "ecumenism." These are the same people they are calling to unity, whom they excommunicated only yesterday. So what will excommunication mean to us? First of all, there are no grounds for excommunication.

The married priests have finally come to understand that the Roman Catholic Church, which has decided to remain adamant in a matter that can be waved off by a simple gesture of the pope, will demand a convening of a council. If so, then we know how little the Church cares about the situation of the married priests. That is why we added "Now," in "Married Priests Now!"

Neither can the Church excommunicate Milingo, because he is just playing the role of a good Samaritan. These priests needed official approval, someone who can guarantee that he is undertaking what he is doing in the name of and by the authority of Jesus. It is not only this matter, which he has to carry out in relation with the Church; there is still something almost equally important on the way. Today let us be satisfied with this matter, which we consider an emergency for the well being of the Church.

The married priests were abandoned, left to fend for themselves. Whatever would befall them was of no concern for the Catholic Church. It is not a new story. So were the old Catholics, the Lutherans, the Calvinists, the Anglicans, the Baptists and many others, some of which have taken the name "National Churches." How do you use those whom you erased from your list as no longer priests as a means to condemn someone who has been moved with compassion to take all possible means to restore to the nature of their priesthood their dignity and sense of belonging to Christ? There is neither logic nor sense of human understanding. I have left all to realize this objective, and the Lord said: "Even if this will demand your life, offer your life, as the others did in the past."

Today I have to hear from you. As you will see in our agenda, we are improving our organization. We have had good advice and we expect more from you today. Once more, I say welcome to all of you.

May God bless us and bless our meeting.

Archbishop E. Milingo

My Dear Married Priests,

I AM PRESENTING TO you my four first bishops and archbishops, who have decided to totally work with me for Married Priests Now! They will have my authority as they come to you. Open up your hearts, as you have done with me through your letters and e-mails. I shall soon announce these to you as we share our pastoral work in order to cover the whole world, wherever you are.

As we meet you, do not dwell too much on your past misery. But rather for the fact that we all have offered our lives to serve you, rest assured that carrying one another's burden will now be a reality. We all, now your bishops, pledge our lives to God in the service of you and of all those whom you too serve.

We appeal to those bishops and archbishops, punished by being hidden in monasteries, to come out and work out their punishment in public, as we are all doing. Condemned we all are and have been, and some of us are still among street children, abandoned by their Mother Church. Though we are not yet big, but being many, we shall see to it that at least you have the necessities of life, such as shelter and food. Pray to St. Joseph to provide us with these things, and I say pray to the Blessed Virgin Mary to teach us her priests, as she says, to be good husbands, to form and lead good families.

I, in my humble capacity as an apostle of Christ, appeal to you to have no more grudges against Mother Church. Present yourself to us, and we shall do all we can to help you in the process of cleansing yourself from the mire of degradation through which you have passed. Attach yourself to our association and learn once more to celebrate Mass. "You are a priest forever." Amen.

Archbishop E. Milingo

Archbishop Emmanuel Milingo at the American Clergy
Leadership Seminar Dinner, NJ, September, 2006.

PART IV

Response to
Bishop George Lungu,
Bishop of Chipata Diocese

August 3, 2006

Right Rev. Bishop George Lungu,

TODAY, ON AUGUST 3, 2006, we have come across your sermon on the occasion of priestly ordination, and conferring of diaconate on August 1, 2006. I sincerely thank you for your prayers, and of those present whom you invited to pray for me. Acknowledging your disappointment, I would like you to change the prayers to married priest, not so much for me.

I will share with you something, which you and I did not know up until now. What I am only superficially sharing with you here needs a full thesis to be put to the Catholic Church, and they may not give an answer. Let me just ask you: "How much does the Catholic Church deserve the title, 'Mother'?" If you will listen to the stories of the married priests about how they have been treated, certainly, if you have any humanity in you, you will not accept that the Catholic Church deserves the title, "Mother."

Let me bring to your knowledge the concept of sex in the Western Christian Churches. Those who have influenced the Western Christian concept of sex are St. Augustine,

St. Jerome and Tertullian. To all three, sex was anathema, and St. Augustine was afraid to become a priest because of celibacy. St. Augustine wept like a child over the fact that in order to embrace the Christian religion, he had to abandon his sexual waywardness. His change of lifestyle was a bitter change of attitude towards sexuality. Let me share with you what Karen Armstrong says of St. Augustine in relation to sexuality:

> Augustine left us with a difficult heritage. A religion, which teaches men and women to regard their humanity as chronically flawed, can alienate them from themselves. Nowhere is this alienation more evident than in the denigration of sexuality in general and women in particular. Even though Christianity had originally been quite positive for women, it had already developed a misogynistic tendency in the West by the time of Augustine. (Karen Armstrong: *The History of God*)

Priests in Western Christianity during their lifetime live holding onto their cherished celibacy, while considering women as the thieves who may rob it away from them. Even their love for women remains platonic, since it should not be manifested in the form of emotions, sensation or sentiments. The love of a celibate priest for a woman is surrounded by precautions not to touch the unholy, a woman being the cause of man's fall.

Speaking of St. Jerome, who went as far as scratching himself with stones in order not to fall into temptation from the sexual urge, Karen Armstrong writes as follows: "The letters of St. Jerome teem with loathing of the female which occasionally sounds deranged."

But there was no woman around him. He was dealing with the words of God, translating the Bible into Latin from Hebrew and Greek. So as St. James says:

> No one experiencing temptation should say, "I am being tempted by God," for God is not subject to temptation to evil, and He Himself tempts no one. Rather each person is tempted when he is lured and enticed by his own desire. (James 1:13-15)

The celibate priest finds it hard to appreciate even innocent gestures of love from a woman. We have all become the disciples of Tertullian, whose fury against women we have inherited, and has been ingrown in us. Here is what he says about women: "Do you not know that you are each an Eve?" What an address to women! He goes on to say:

> The sentence of God on this sex of yours lives in this age. The guilt must of necessity live too. You are the devil's gateway; you are the unsealer of that forbidden tree; you are the first deserter of the divine law; you are "she" who persuaded him (Adam) whom the devil was not valiant enough to attack. You so carelessly destroyed man, God's image. On account of your desert, even the Son of God had to die. (Karen Armstrong: *The History of God*)

Can the Catholic Church get away with it as easily as that? My Lord Bishop G. Lungu, respect me as you have so far done. I am not out of my wits. The positive responses from our first document have been such that we cannot turn back. We are not asking for abolition of celibacy. Our future married priests will not look down on women, but consider them as a fulfillment of mankind in the divine plans. They are the essence of the totality of humanity. Thus says Karen Armstrong:

> A religion which looks askance upon half the human race and which regards every involuntary motion of mind, heart and body as a symptom of fatal concupiscence can only alienate men and women from their condition. Western Christianity never fully recovered from this neurotic misogyny, which can still be seen in the unbalanced reaction to the very notion of the ordination of women.

May I ask you, my lord, to analyze the following words of St. Augustine: "What is the difference," he wrote to a friend, "whether it is a wife or a mother; it is still Eve the temptress that we must beware of in any woman."

St. Augustine does not agree with God for having created a woman as a companion to man: "It would have been much better arranged to have two men together as friends, not a man and a woman." He forgot about procreation to fill the earth with holy souls, from a pure couple, Adam and Eve. Adam as the firstborn failed to question "flesh from his flesh," when he saw her with an evil proposal. It was all in his hands to say no "to my own child whom I bore from my ribs." He failed God; he did not take his responsibility. He is the one who is a lot more at fault. God had strongly whispered into his ears about the way to live in Eden, in the midst of such possible attractive fruits. He disappointed God the more. That is why God first looked for him and questioned him on the matter.

Consequently, the more celibacy stands out as a man's victory over sex, while looking down on women, it has no merits. The humiliations from the defaulters of celibacy should teach the Catholic Church the normality of a human being. Sex is no more a bitter fruit. There is no one-sided condemnation by pointing fingers to women.

They are made in God's image, and as such they deserve respect and dignity. They are not just sex objects; they are persons, the indwelling of God, the Triune God. Please, my lord bishop, understand us.

We wish the best for the Church.

Yours most respectfully,

Archbishop Emmanuel Milingo

PART V

Vatican Intervention and Milingo's Response

Congretio Pro Episcopis

CANONICAL ADMONITION

For the Most Reverend Emmanuel Milingo, Archbishop Emeritus of Lusaka

SUMMARY

Cardinal Re, Prefect of the Congregation of Bishops, sent Archbishop Emmanuel Milingo a letter dated September 8, 2006, stating that his behaviors, actions and public statements contrary to his obligation as a Bishop showed that he was unfaithful to the doctrines and disciplines of the Church. This caused the entire Church confusion, scandal and pain:

- Establishing and becoming head of "Married Priests Now," which calls for priests who have married to exercise sacred ministry.

- Inviting those priests to celebrate the Eucharist and then organizing and presiding over such Eucharistic celebrations with some of those priests.
- Initiating a close relationship with the "African-American Catholic Congregation," which although it has "catholic" in its title is not in reality part of the Catholic Church.

The letter reminded Archbishop Milingo of his grave responsibility as a Bishop of the Catholic Church to promote and defend the unity of the church's doctrine, worship and discipline, especially in celebrating the Eucharist and in the ministry of the Word.

Expressing confidence that he would repent, Cardinal Re implored Archbishop Milingo to renounce the above positions and send a written declaration of repentance by October 15, 2006. Otherwise, he would be subject to punishment of canonical suspension, which would prohibit all acts of power of order and of jurisdiction.

Each of the statements included references to canonical law.

The admonition concluded with a plea in the name of Jesus Christ for Archbishop Milingo to reflect seriously on his behavior and all its consequences.

Cardinal Re
Prefect of the Congregation of Bishops

Vatican City, Vatican
Our Dearly Beloved Brother Bishop, Cardinal Re:

THE MARRIED PRIESTS NOW! Association takes this opportunity to respond to your letter to Archbishop Milingo which indicates that he will be suspended for his work with married priests. We thank you for your gracious care and concern for his work and ministry.

As you have asked, together with Archbishop Milingo we have reflected on the extent and meaning of the Archbishop's work among married priests. It is clear to His Excellency that, led by the Holy Spirit, he is more than ever fulfilling his responsibilities as a bishop of the Church. What is the Church if it is not the place of forgiveness and reconciliation, especially for those who have suffered so long from the unjust treatment at the hands of the bureaucracy of the Church?

Archbishop Milingo is and remains a bishop of the Roman Catholic Church. It is our hope that he will continue to minister to the People of God, especially to the married priests who are called to serve and who yearn for the consolation of the Church.

The current shortage of priests is at an emergency level. Because of this crisis, we request that married priests be reconciled and reinstated to full service in the Church. They are available, trained and more than eager to serve.

Your Brothers in Christ,

Archbishop Peter P. Brennan
Archbishop Joseph J. Gouthro
Archbishop Patrick E. Trujillo
Archbishop George A. Stallings

ARCHBISHOP MILINGO'S PRESS STATEMENT IN RESPONSE TO THE VATICAN CENSURE

WE CORDIALLY THANK THE Holy Father for his gracious and caring concern about us and our College of Bishops and the Prelature for Married Priests Now! It is our intention to be faithful to the Church and to honor and respect the Holy Father. We thank him for his brotherly love and we hope to return the same to him.

We do have a grave concern about the lives of our married priests who have been dismissed from service in the Church because they have married. And we wish to speak about that injustice.

The purpose of the Married Priests Now! Personal Prelature is to support the priests who have married and to loudly clamor for their return to full ministry in the Church. We have only one goal and purpose and that is the restoration of the married priesthood to the Western Roman Catholic Church. To support married priests I, Archbishop Emmanuel Milingo, a married Roman Catholic bishop, last July held a press conference in the Press Club of Washington, D.C., to point out the growing crisis in the priesthood. The average age of priests is approximately 74, and the average age of male and female religious is 68. In twenty years, there will be few priests left. Who is going to provide the sacraments and the Eucharist to the people?

Churches are closing at the rate of almost fifty a year in the larger cities in the United States. There is a desperate need for priests now and in the future, but we have almost 25,000 married priests in the U.S. and almost 150,000 worldwide who are not being called to service because the Medieval Church imposed a regulation that priests be celibate. The sexual abuse accusations against celibate priests in the United States speak loudly that something is wrong. And what is wrong is the enforcement of a promise of celibacy on the priests. Secular clergy should be married so that they can model what a good family is in the church community and so they can relate to the families they serve. We also pointed out the brutal and unacceptable treatment the Church has imposed on those priests who fell in love and married. That same week a second press conference was held at Imani Temple to accommodate the interest of the international press. Earlier this month we held a convocation with 120 married priests and their wives.

Married Priests Now! is drawing attention to the great need for priests due to the present shortage of priests which is creating a crisis in the Roman Catholic Church. More than 150,000 married priests stand waiting and willing to serve the needs of the Church. These men are already trained and experienced in theology and ministry and have many years experience as married men. These are men who have loved their wives and raised families. They ought to be called back to ministry immediately. The very life of the Church is at stake. Without priests, there is no Mass or Eucharist. The Eucharist is the center of the Catholic-Christian experience and faith; no Eucharist, no church.

The Church has always had married priests. It was the norm of the Church for twelve centuries to have married priests and, in the early centuries, married bishops and popes. Thirty-nine popes were married. In our own day, the Eastern Rites of the Roman Catholic Church have married priests. In the United States, in the last thirty years because of what is known as the Pastoral Provision, there are about 70 married priests who transferred from Anglican and Lutheran churches. The married priesthood is already here. We are calling for an extension of this Pastoral Provision for our own married priests.

We celebrate the married priests of the Roman Catholic Church. Up to this time, the priests who married were punished, penalized and shunned by the Roman Catholic hierarchy. We want the laity to join us and to courageously call upon the Vatican to remove these unjust penalties and to stop the unchristian retaliation towards married priests. We call on the Holy Father to recall in dignity and honor the priests who have married. Marriage is a sacrament and is a higher calling than celibacy. This is a matter of discernment for the whole Church, and the laity must be involved in seeing the need for married priests. We honor and celebrate the married priests of the Roman Catholic Church, and we will work closely with the Holy Father, the Vatican offices and other married priest organizations to once again make a married priesthood a normal part of the Church. We celebrate the married priesthood. All of our voices need to be one chorus of celebration for the priests who have chosen to find love and marry. They are better priests because of it.

Now we turn our attention to the charges made by the Vatican about the consecration of our four married bishops. When I, as a Roman Catholic bishop, decided to consecrate four bishops, I meditated and went back to the roots of the apostolic times and reviewed what the apostles had done. They set up spiritual leaders in the church communities by praying and laying hands on them. They did not look for mandates but for the needs of the communities. I have done the same thing. I consecrated these four married men as Roman Catholic bishops in valid apostolic succession. The power and authority of a bishop comes from the very power and authority of his own sacramental consecration. I was consecrated by Pope Paul VI and, equipped with that sacramental power from him, I consecrated four married men in valid apostolic succession. These men are validly ordained Roman Catholic bishops today and remain so in spite of Rome's posture of denial of recognition.

The canon cited in the excommunication says I acted without a papal mandate. There have been many times before in Church history when mandates were not required, and the current priest shortage calls for emergency action to bring attention and remedy to the problem. The Gospel calls us to do what is right. This may appear to the canon lawyer to be an illicit consecration, but in terms of the Gospel of Jesus Christ, it is the right thing to do. These bishops are both valid and licit.

We do not accept this excommunication and lovingly return it to His Holiness, our beloved Pope Benedict XVI, to reconsider it and withdraw it and join us in recalling married priests to service once again. We call upon the bishops of dioceses to bring back the married priests because they have long been needed to do the work of the Church. Lay people need to write to the bishops and to the newspapers to tell them to return married priests to ministry.

We are and continue to be dedicated to the unity of the Church. We are calling back those who have been disowned by the Church and providing them with healing and acceptance. This is great ministry and we act out of care for the Church and for its survival. We will continue with our mission, and we ask the laity and the married priests to join us.

OCTOBER 10, 2006

His Holiness Pope Benedict XVI
00120 Vatican City, Rome

Most Holy Father,
Peace of Christ.

PRAYING FOR YOU MEANS praying for the Catholic Church. Rest assured, Most Holy Father, that this is for me as a parental duty, which emanates from the parents to their children. That is, to owe love and respect to parents. Doing so on the part of the children is to their own advantage, because the welfare of the parents is advantageous to their children. Hence, praying for you, Most Holy Father, is praying for myself, because I know that you have all of us in your heart.

The many married priests look to me as to their elder brother, who leads them back to their Mother Church. So many capable priests who were detached from the Catholic Church through an offence against celibacy founded many churches. They retained the name Catholic, but not Roman Catholic. Many of them went in search of Episcopal consecration to Old Catholic bishops, or to the Orthodox, like those in Ukraine.

However, they are now looking to me for consecration under the condition that they be reunited with the Catholic Church. As a matter of fact, that looks like something unacceptable externally, but in the end all the roads lead to Rome. One day I will organize a pilgrimage to Rome of married priests and bishops, if Your Holiness has no objection.

We will have ordination of priests on December 9 and consecration of bishops on December 10, 2006. Old Catholic bishops have consecrated these bishops. They want to be certain that they are in line with St. Peter's apostolicity. How long they have been waiting for this opportunity!

This week's schedule is as follows. We will leave Washington, D.C., on October 12 and will return on October 19, 2006. I am coming back to my original mission: preaching the Gospel, casting out devils, and healing the sick. We shall move as follows:

1. October 13 - Los Angeles
2. October 15 - Phoenix
3. October 18 - San Francisco

May the glory of the Lord manifest itself, and win the many people who find hope in our mission. All in Jesus' name and His Catholic Church.

I am in contact with Cardinal Cheli for any developments.

Counting on your Paternal blessing and prayers.

Your obedient servant,

Archbishop Emmanuel Milingo

September 6, 2006

His Eminence Cardinal Giovanni Cheli
00120 Vatican City, Rome

Your Eminence, Cardinal Giovani Cheli,

I AM HEREBY THANKING you for the kind wishes you sent me on my priestly ordination anniversary. It is through the prayers and sacrifices of many who love me that I have been able to remain a priest during the hard moments of my priestly life. Certainly, your prayers feature in the high atmosphere of God's providence. I am conscious of what you say, "To remain within the Catholic Church." I take that very seriously. I take courage from the Fathers of the Church, who had such faith that their whole lives were permeated with God's will, and like Jesus, they were truly able to say: "I came to do the will of my Father."

Mine is a hard vocation. Just as I have not been understood, so do I not understand myself. Not because I don't want to, but the nature of the things I know do not permit me to be so lavish in sharing my spiritual experiences. "Once beaten, twice shy." This fact developed within me "a go it alone attitude." As to what I am undertaking this time, it is so clear to me that I cannot withdraw my efforts to help the married priests.

It seems contradictory to embark on realizing one good thing at the cost of destroying an already well-established good work, my three congregations. But they are in the good hands of the mother Church. But most of what we call the life of the mystical body in the Catholic Church is hinged on the priest's life. For this reason, a priest is called "father" because he is the fountain, which distributes divine life in the Catholic Church through the sacraments. The Catholic Church in a desperate situation has tried to make sacerdotal services available by multiplying deacons, married deacons, permanent deacons and Eucharistic ministers. All these modes of half priests, quarter priests, or whatever divisions they may split into, cannot take the place of one valid priest, who is *"alter Christus."* They cannot call God to come down on the altar, because they are not called like Melchizedek, the eternal priest, who preceded Jesus, God-man, by divine appointment as "The High Priest."

Our priesthood derived from the eternal priesthood of Jesus is valid forever and will remain so in eternity. A precept introduced as the luster of the Church and for many side reasons, celibacy has turned in the course of time into a killer of the priests' pastoral ministry, at the cost of depriving many Catholic communities of their daily spiritual food.

Is it a small matter to see a mother who totally loses interest in a baby do an abominable action such as throwing it away into a garbage can? Have the priests who have married not been treated likewise? The Catholic Church has publicly declared "To hell with you. We have no more interest in you." Some of these priests having had only ecclesiastical qualifications to serve the Church, when they went into the world they had to start from scratch. The Catholic Church refused even to give them a testimonial for resettlement in the world. Thank God, since some have been in contact with us, they are once more able to pronounce the word "Catholic."

What have they all done in all to satisfy themselves? Convinced that they are forever priests, some of them have founded their own churches. And some others have joined other churches, churches that either are separated from or condemned by the Catholic Church. Others have formed consolation associations of people who come together as children left alone when their mother has been taken away from them by sudden death. How long will the Catholic Church play the Levite and the priest of the parable of the Good Samaritan, who pass by, leaving the wounded as someone untouchable?

It has never dawned in my mind to abolish celibacy. I am too small to do that. I see it more and more as an option to any candidate to priesthood. The value of priesthood is inherent in its nature, as the Fathers of the Church say:

O venerable and sacred dignity of priests, in whose hands, as in the womb of the Virgin, the Son of God is incarnate every day, O stupendous mystery which God the Father and the Son and the Holy Ghost perform through the priest in so wonderful a manner. (St. Augustine: *Sermo de dignitate sacerdotum*)

St. John Damascene has this to say:

Should anyone ask, "How is the bread changed into the body of Christ?" I answer: "The Holy Ghost overshadows the priest and operates through him that which He operated in the sacred womb of Mary." (Lib. 2, C. 14)

St. John Chrysostom said:

Heaven has nothing, absolutely nothing more than earth; the earth has become a new Heaven. Go up to the gates of Heaven, or rather go up to the highest Heaven; look attentively, and I will afterward show you an altar that which struck you more than anything else in Paradise.

Aware of their priestly dignity, even when they have been put by force on the shelf, they die desiring "to say at least one Mass before I die. If not, I hope that one day things will be put right." Another priest goes on living in concubinage for fear that by becoming a married priest he will no more minister in the Catholic Church. I am sending the letter of Paola, through which finally we have learned what the wives of married priests go through.

THE NECESSITY OF THE AVAILABILITY OF THE PRIESTS

No place on the earth is dearer to devout Christians than a church where the sacrifice of the Mass is daily celebrated. In the mere remembrance of the divine mysteries, they find assistance in the great combat of life. (Father Michael

Muller, C.S.S.R.: *The Holy Sacrifice of the Mass*)

Let the Mass come back and take its original place in the life of the Catholic Church. As we fight for married priesthood, we are at the same time fighting for the return of one hundred and fifty thousand (150,000) missed Masses.

Your blessing, Your Eminence.

Yours devotedly,

Archbishop E. Milingo

His Eminence Cardinal Giovanni Cheli
00120 Vatican City, Rome

Your Eminence, Cardinal Giovani Cheli,
Peace of Christ.

THIS IS AN E-MAIL. As I did the other week, I shall forward to you our material for the next meeting to be held September 17-19. I would have loved to send these items to the Holy Father. But due to the many hands through which they may pass, I have restrained myself from doing so.

I have added in the collection of my circulars and some statements, including a letter to you. It is the only way to give hope to the married priests that we are in communion with the Church. They truly want to resume their priestly ministry. I have invited them to come and celebrate, and they look forward to this fact with joy.

There have emerged many small churches founded by married priests, some of which bear the name: "Catholic Ecumenical Church." It means any denomination may join them in worship. When they now look at me, they have hope that they will truly be Catholic since I am in communion with the Catholic Church. This hope founded in me has made me feel such a responsibility that I have been totally disarmed. I saw before me something more serious than I ever conceived before.

One Anglican priest, to whom we went to borrow a thurible, knowing as he greeted me that I have been consecrated by the Pope, said: "Finally I hope you will put right my priestly ordination." They have the presence of Jesus in their churches. They still receive communion traditionally, kneeling on altar rails.

In Brazil and Peru we have two bishops who have more than 5,000 married priests. The one from Brazil is coming, while the one from Peru will be present at the next meeting. That is why you will see in my circulars that I don't deviate from the teaching of the Church. Nobody wants any more to be called ex-Catholic. With my being with the Church, they expect finally to be fully incorporated in the Catholic Church. The Unification Church has never experienced such world influence with one public declaration. They have observed that the Catholic Church has its own language. Not even those priests who joined them in the past ever dreamt of forming an international body such as ours: "Married Priests Now!" Thus, we have no interference from them. We have an organization committee, which has met more than four times organizing the forthcoming meeting.

In Italy we are better organized in the North:

1. Bergamo
2. Milan

3. Torino
4. Rimini
5. Naples

Germany, Holland and Belgium are looking on, while Switzerland and Austria just go their own way.

Your Eminence, you may look at my mapping of Europe as an exaggeration. You will see when I shall begin to move. The married priests will be a power for the Catholic Church, and they love the Catholic Church.

The two strange categories of people who have approached us have made us be on the alert as to what kind of men we are dealing with: the homosexual priests and the married men who failed to pursue their priestly vocation due to obligatory celibacy. We did not expect this. However, we have come to realize the value of priesthood in the mind of a Catholic.

Let me not forget to thank Msgr. Pinto, who started a novena on September 8 for me. The novena ends exactly on the opening of the meeting. This is a very important meeting for us. This time we shall have more bishops. Of course, the majority are married priests.

We are in touch with the whole world. That is why I have been obliged to write three circulars in less than two months. Put us in your prayers, your Eminence.

Yours most respectfully,

Archbishop E. Milingo

AN OPEN LETTER TO HIS HOLINESS POPE BENEDICT XVI ON RESCINDING MANDATORY CELIBACY

From the Married Priests Now! Prelature

October 23, 2006

Your Holiness,

THE ARCHBISHOPS, BISHOPS AND Priests of the Married Priests Now! Prelature send their cordial greetings to you and to the Cardinals, Archbishops and Bishops of the Church.

As you know, the Church throughout the world is in dire straits because of the shortage of priests. Churches are closing, priests are serving two and three parishes, the Mass and the Eucharist is not available to hundreds of thousands of Catholics. Lay men and women are being appointed as canonical pastors of parishes. The church-at-large has become a mission territory.

In the face of this crisis, there are 150,000 married priests who are ready and willing to serve. And there are married men who have prepared themselves for ordination who can also be called to the priesthood. Some of them are currently married deacons but others have never been ordained at all.

The Married Priests Now! Prelature with its archbishops, bishops and priests considers itself to be a Roman Catholic Personal Prelature in communion with Your Holiness and is part of the Roman Catholic Church. We are Roman Catholic bishops and do not want to fracture the communion of the Church. Our cause is great because it is for the survival of the Church. We are mature adults, not children, so threats, penalties and punishments are out of place in our conversation and will not work. What will work is an honest discussion about the married priesthood of the New Testament and of the primitive Church. The faithful are already reaching out daily to married priests for weddings, baptisms and funerals on a continuing basis. It is time to free the priesthood from the obligation of celibacy.

This is what needs to be done without delay:

1. Married priests and married bishops need to be immediately but gradually reinstated into the fabric of our Church. A vicariate or prelature can be established for married priests (and there was a precedent for this in progress under John Paul II) or they can be recalled through our Married Priests Now! Prelature, or recalled by the local bishops. All penalties need to be waived.

2. Married deacons who are trained in theology and ministry ought to be ordained to the priesthood within a year or two.

3. Married men who are not ordained need to be welcomed into the seminaries or other training programs for the priesthood within the year.

4. Married priests should be able to serve in full-time positions with salary, health care plans and pensions or in part-time positions. Credit towards pensions should be given for past service to the Church.

5. Marriage is a sacrament of the Church. It cannot be said that celibacy is higher or greater than the sacrament of marriage. Marriage is the higher calling and is more difficult than celibacy because it is naturally centered on the spouse and children. Marriage creates great holiness in the husband and wife and in the family. Married priests' families are a model of the Christian family for the other families in the parish.

   Marriage does not diminish the priest's dedication to Christ but enhances it.

6. We wish to keep the avenues of communication and contact with you open, Your Holiness, and with the other bishops for our Married Priests Now! Prelature.

The priests and bishops of the Married Priests Now! Prelature stand ready and willing to work with you. The Faithful of the Church are now already reaching out to married priests in an enormous way. A new Catholic Church is forming with or without your blessing. There is great urgency in this matter. If you sanction this approach to reinstating married priests and bishops, you will be preserving the unity of the church. The right time is now.

We ask your cordial blessing on all married priests and bishops.

With filial love and devotion,

Emmanuel Milingo
Peter Paul Brennan
Joseph J. Gouthro
Patrick E. Trujillo
George Augustus Stallings
Roman Catholic Archbishops
The Married Priests Now! Prelature

A similar open letter has been mailed to the president and simultaneously to every member of the United States Conference of Catholic Bishops.

CONCLUDING REMARKS

What Is in Store for Married Priests?

WITHIN ALL MY CIRCULARS I can see the Roman Catholic Church full of priests in the now empty parishes. To come to this end, the Church must have courage to ask pardon from the so many sex scandal victims. On the other hand, the Church must be humble enough to acknowledge its lack of vision and take preventive measures to avoid what has been happening within the Church, which has taken them so long to do.

On our part as married priests, once reinstated, we have no reason to fall back into the wiles of the evil one. Our chastity will now be maintained by the intertwined strings of love which will be supplied by the two persons now officially married. So shall our priesthood not be the business of one man but of the whole family.

Archbishop E. Milingo

Biography of Emmanuel Milingo

Archbishop Emmanuel Milingo, Roman Catholic archbishop and former bishop of Lusaka, Zambia, rose from humble beginnings to stand at the center of a bitter controversy affecting the future of the Roman Catholic faith and the definition of its priesthood.

Born in 1930 in a poor farming village in Zambia's Eastern Province, Milingo, a member of the Ngoni tribe, was raised in the warrior tradition. At age 12 this illiterate cattle herder, who spoke only his tribal language and had never been outside his own village, ran away to enter a mission school. Within two years he could read and speak English and began his seminary education. Ordained a priest in 1958, he obtained diplomas in sociology in Rome and education in Dublin, served his local Chipata parish from 1963-66 and founded the Zambia Helper's Society, a humanitarian organization, to bring health care to the shantytowns.

Called to Lusaka, the nation's capital, as an assistant for communications to the Zambian Episcopal Conference in 1966, Milingo's radio ministry made him a popular national figure. He founded the first of three orders, the Daughters of the Redeemer, in 1969. Pope Paul VI consecrated him Archbishop of the diocese of Lusaka, as one of Africa's youngest bishops. He served there from 1969 to 1983.

Archbishop Milingo experienced the reality of the spirit world, and came to confront the spiritual power of evil, becoming known as an exorcist. He developed a charismatic healing ministry, and increasingly people flocking to healing services at the cathedral and lined the stairs at his home. In 1976 he joined the Catholic charismatic renewal movement that was spreading throughout the church, finding a spiritual link between his African heritage and his conservative Catholic faith.

The increasingly popular archbishop became a champion of inculturation: the development of an authentic African Christianity expressed through indigenous spiritual and cultural symbols. Seeking to validate the religious experience of native Africans and to overcome a colonial mentality, he challenged Western control of the African church and its European cultural expressions. More than simply using local languages or including traditional dancing in services, he began Africanizing institutions, practices, and attitudes, making many foreign missionaries uncomfortable. He set up women's councils at all levels and fostered grassroots Basic Christian Communities. He continued his social reforms and denounced the wealthy African elite for commercialism and exploiting the poor, seeking to foster a religious and spiritual renewal.

Accused of practicing witchcraft and promoting heresy, Milingo was barred from holding healing services in 1979, and recalled to Rome in 1982. He was forced to resign as Bishop of Lusaka and reassigned to a minor post on the Vatican Commission for Migration and Tourism. But more importantly, Pope John Paul II recognized the African healer's charism, and promised to protect it. Soon European Catholics were equally inspired, flocking to healing services held in Rome, throughout Italy, and in other countries. This caused continued tension with diocesan leaders, and year-by-year, Milingo's freedom to hold mass and perform healings was further restricted.

Appealing to Christ's original charge to his disciples, Milingo consistently explained that he was only fulfilling the Lord's call to "heal the sick, cast out demons, and preach the gospel." He lamented that it was his own beloved church that was preventing him from heeding this call. He became an outspoken critic of spiritual and moral corruption within the Vatican, claiming even the presence of Satan within the curia. He lamented the moral decline of the priesthood, charging that the church was tolerating violations of clerical celibacy and all manner of sexual sins among clerics, threatening the sanctity of the priesthood and the moral integrity of the Church.

Seeing no contradiction between his fervent Catholic faith and a commitment to ecumenism, Archbishop Milingo became a participant and supporter of the interreligious work of Reverend and Mrs. Sun Myung Moon. In May 2001, he wed Maria Sung, a 43 year-old Korean acupuncturist in a Marriage Blessing Ceremony with 60 clergy couples from various faiths, officiated by Rev. and Mrs. Moon. He announced that his decision to marry was not out of desire or emotion, but to confront the growing immorality that had infected the priesthood through the corruption of celibacy. He pointed out that Jesus had ordained Peter, who was married, as the first pope, and that the Bible quotes Paul encouraging bishops to marry "only once." He noted that while marriage is a sacrament in the church, celibacy is but an administrative rule enacted eleven centuries after Christ. Moreover, he professed his wholehearted Catholic faith and undying love for the Church.

Naturally, the archbishop's marriage was considered invalid by the Vatican, to whom it seemed that he had violated his vows and converted to another faith. Threatened with excommunication, Milingo returned to Rome with his wife months later, seeking an audience with Pope John Paul II. At the urging of the Holy Father he reportedly set his marriage aside, but his subsequent disappearance, year-long seclusion and quiet return left many questions unanswered. He continued his healing ministry in Zagarolo, outside of Rome. After four long years of constant observation and restrictive supervision, during which he secretly maintained communication with Maria Sung, he has again emerged to challenge the conscience of the Church he loves.

Affirming once again the sanctity of marriage and its importance in promoting a healthy and whole priesthood, Milingo proclaims that celibacy must be a gift of the spirit, not an administrative mandate. On July 12, 2006, he founded "Married Priests Now!" as an "independent charismatic ministry to reconcile married priests with the Catholic Faith." With growing support from among the nearly 150,000 married priests worldwide, he ordained four married clerics as bishops on September 24, 2006. Two days later the Vatican announced that this act resulted in automatic excommunication for Milingo and his bishops, an assertion refuted by the Archbishop and supporters worldwide. This book documents the ongoing story.